I0062152

PERSONAL FINANCE

For Your 20'S

YOUR 20'S YOUR WEALTH: MASTER MONEY MANAGEMENT
REAL WORLD STRATEGIES TO CREATE FINANCIAL CONFIDENCE
UNLOCK WEALTH AND FREEDOM TODAY!

WILLIAM P. BURKE

© Copyright 2023 - All rights reserved.

ISBN: 979-8-86-281789-8 (paperback)
ISBN: 979-8-86-315886-0 (hardcover)

The content contained within this book may not be reproduced, duplicated or
transmitted without direct written permission from the author or the publisher.

Under no circumstances will any blame or legal responsibility be held against the publisher, or
author, for any damages, reparation, or monetary loss due to the information contained within this
book. Either directly or indirectly. You are responsible for your own choices, actions, and results.

Legal Notice:
This book is copyright protected. This book is only for personal use. You
cannot amend, distribute, sell, use, quote or paraphrase any part, or the content
within this book, without the consent of the author or publisher.

Disclaimer Notice:
Please note the information contained within this document is for educational purposes only. All effort
has been executed to present accurate, up to date, and reliable, complete information. No warranties of
any kind are declared or implied. Readers acknowledge that the author is not engaging in the rendering of
legal, financial, medical or professional advice. The content within this book has been derived from various
sources. Please consult a licensed professional before attempting any techniques outlined in this book.

By reading this document, the reader agrees that under no circumstances is the author responsible
for any losses, direct or indirect, which are incurred as a result of the use of the information
contained within this document, including, but not limited to, errors, omissions, or inaccuracies.

CONTENTS

INTRODUCTION

---

*L*ife in your 20's is pretty fun, full, rich, and at the same time, chaotic. This is when you move out on your own, kick off your career, and get to know yourself better. There will be mistakes made and opportunities lost, but all the other things in between will really make you realize that in the end, life is what you make of it.

One big part of being in your 20's is developing good habits that you can keep throughout the rest of your years. This book will focus on the financial habits that you can create early in life. After all, we all know that it's better and easier to develop good habits early than correct bad ones later on!

This book will teach you how to be intimate with your money and with your life decisions in general. We'll start by identifying where you are and talk about the rest of the ways to master personal finance in your 20's. From learning how to save, budget, get out of debt, and build wealth.... you're in for a real treat!

This time in your life is crucial, and I would like to congratulate you for grabbing this type of book and learning about personal finance aimed at financial freedom. It shows how committed you are to doing 'adulting' right and shaping the life you deserve. The money decisions that you'll make now will affect your finances for the years to come.

How you handle your finances today will make or break your financial destiny. It also dictates whether or not you'll have a smooth glide to adulthood or a rocky, stressful one. Money mistakes can affect both your mental and physical health. In the end, it's not just about having money, but it's about securing your well-being and making sure that you keep the best currencies out there: peace of mind and freedom.

When you're young, you have the advantage of time. We'll discuss later on in the book why it's crucial to start early and how the power of time and compound interest can help you amass the fortune you deserve down the road.

This moment is all about new adventures and big life decisions, and I'm here to help. Let's start building the financial foundation that your future self will thank you for!

Chapter 1

WHERE DID ALL MY MONEY GO?

Y ou remember working hard, being exhausted, and occasionally losing motivation and the will to live. However, you can no longer recall where all your hard-earned money went. You look back on months or even years of work with nothing to show for it, and you're sick of this recurring theme. You're done being broke, and you're ready to finally bring order to chaos.

In the US alone, living paycheck to paycheck has become a way of life. Only 49% of Americans have at least $1000 in savings, and 34% have no savings at all.[1] Around 25% of Americans rely on credit cards to pay their bills, and 54% feel like they can't get ahead of their finances and are constantly experiencing financial stress.

If you're one of the many people struggling to keep their finances together, the best way to address the situation is to analyze your financial position and take a hard look at your spending habits. In this chapter, we will uncover the deepest reasons behind your financial struggles, the psychology behind your spending habits, and the financial mistakes you should avoid to turn the tide and achieve the financial freedom and security you deserve.

ANALYZING YOUR FINANCIAL POSITION

The first step to solving any problem is to acknowledge that there is a problem. The best way to acknowledge your problem is to examine all the minutiae. Before you fine-tune your finances, do a quick inventory of all your financial instruments and analyze where you are on this journey.

The list below contains the key financial metrics you should be looking at to start analyzing your financial position.

Net worth

If there's only one metric to follow for measuring one's financial health, it would be one's net worth. Net worth is simply **assets - liabilities**. It is the ultimate reflection of the financial decisions you made in the past. It shows your performance in making, saving, and investing money. *Your income is not the key measure of your financial stability— it's your net worth.* In the next chapters, I will discuss at length how to slowly but surely grow your net worth and set your finances in the right direction.

Debt levels

Carrying bad debt will always threaten your ability to achieve financial security. The longer you carry debts, the more interest you'll have to pay. One of the first steps to financial independence is to pay off debt, and this book dedicates an entire chapter to debt elimination.

Retirement planning

Another key metric for analyzing your financial situation is retirement planning. Are you contributing the maximum allowable amount to IRA, 401k, and other retirement accounts? It's never too early or too late to plan retirement. Again, there will be a whole chapter in this book on the most important retirement planning strategies you should employ to shape your current and future lifestyle and get on top of your finances.

Savings

It's not about how much you earn but how much you save. The amount of savings you have is a key indicator of your financial health. Unfortunately, more and more people are burdened by financial problems, and personal finance is usually viewed as something complex or strenuous. When in fact, *the core formula in personal finance is pretty basic—live below your means, spend less than your income, and save the rest.* What makes this formula impossible to follow is the poor spending habits that people struggle to break. In the next few pages, we'll talk more about assessing your spending habits and getting to the bottom of your relationship with money.[37]

Education

Another key financial metric is financial literacy. The more you understand financial concepts, strategies, and tools, the better equipped you are to optimize your finances effectively. From risk management to debt elimination to investment knowledge, it all starts with your willingness to learn what you ought to learn to avoid financial mistakes and make informed decisions that can transform your life for the better.

Investments

You cannot exponentially build financial freedom without making the right investment decisions. Investing is the core fundamental of wealth building and long-term financial success. Be it stocks, bonds, businesses, or real estate, you need to build and diversify your investment portfolio while managing risks. Build passive income to generate both time and money freedom in the long run.

ASSESSING YOUR SPENDING

The root cause of many people's financial problems is the inability to properly budget and manage their spending habits. Only 32% of Americans keep a household budget and despite high inflation, Americans still spend like crazy.[2]

While it's okay to spend some of your hard-earned money for some well-deserved reward, how much is too much? How do you properly assess your spending habits and where do you draw the line between rewarding yourself now and taking care of your future?

Here's how to start:

1. **Take a closer look at your spending patterns.** The best way to start is to check your credit card history in the past few months. You'll then quickly see where your money is going. Even the little random purchases add up, and unless you start being more mindful about your expenses and budgeting, you'll perpetually ask the question "Where did all my money go?".

2. **Record your current monthly budget that reflects your current spending.** The best way to accurately assess your current spending habits is to know the exact status quo. When drawing up your *as-is monthly budget*, be as thorough as you can. Include the "miscellaneous" category including the tire replacement, your workmate's wedding, and even your savings contributions for your emergency fund or savings account. It's all about income allocation, so look back over the past few months, and jot down everything including medical expenses, insurance payments, tuition, vacation— everything.

3. **Add up the categories recorded and compare the sum to your take-home pay.** This is where you'll find out whether you're actually living within your means or setting yourself up for financial disaster.

I cannot stress enough the importance of having financial control, and *budgeting is the very core of financial stability.* It's so important that I have allocated an entire chapter on how to budget guilt-free. This book will cover everything you need to know to maintain financial stability, reach your financial goals, and achieve financial freedom! To get to the root of your spending habits, it's important to delve into the psychology behind your money issues.

PSYCHOLOGICAL REASONS FOR YOUR MONEY PROBLEMS

Every money problem has an emotional root, and to gain clarity and address your worst money problems, it's important to understand yourself and the deeper problems that are driving your behavior. Your money challenges may stem from one or more of the following psychological burdens:

Fear of repeating the past

The roots of this one could come from growing up in a household where financial mismanagement or instability was the norm. Your beliefs and behaviors around money result from what you witnessed with your parents or guardians. If you have deeply internalized these past experiences, you'll not only fear repeating the same circumstances but you'll end up fearing failure in general. When you fear failure, you'll feel paralyzed, unable to take risks or pursue opportunities that could benefit your financial situation. Ask yourself, "What is holding me back?" and "How can I make better choices moving forward?". I encourage you to write down the answers next to your *as-is budget* from above.

A scarcity mindset

A big sign that you're stuck in the 'scarcity mindset' is if you gravitate towards the feeling of 'lack'. Even if you have material abundance around you, if you always come from a place of 'not enough', you'll always suffer the gnawing feeling of scarcity, the discomfort of feeling like you don't have enough and never will.

Are you feeling constantly anxious about your finances even if you are making and saving enough money? Are you always threatened by competition and comparison? Do you find yourself hating other people's wins? If you answer yes to at least one of these questions, you may have a scarcity mindset problem to address. All those feelings stem from the assumption that there isn't enough going around for everyone and that other people's success takes away a portion of yours. It's like you view the world's rewards like a whole cake and other people who succeed take a slice of the scarce treat when in fact, each one of us can have our own entire cake. You don't need to be threatened by other people acquiring more because you have all the opportunities to write your very own success story!

Unless you learn to deeply understand the problem of scarcity mentality and unless you are resolved to ditch this problematic mindset, you cannot fully embrace the joyful world of the abundance mentality. The abundance mindset is the opposite of the scarcity mindset. It's rooted in the belief that there are enough successes and resources for everyone to share. It's about focusing on your own path and being grateful for the small wins you collect along the way. It's about shaping a better future while embracing the beauty and abundance of today. It's seeing the glass half full instead of half empty. It's allowing yourself to feel plentiful, creative, and inspired. It's about feeling confident and secure in your own personal endeavors and having the clarity to pursue your goals while savoring the present.

Low self-esteem

One of the primary root causes of overspending is low self-esteem. It's the willingness to go broke to look good and confident. It's building your facade to hide the mess and uncertainty underneath. Don't get me wrong. Not everyone who tries to look good has low self-esteem. Fashion can be a genuine art form and genuine self-care. However, pursuing glorious external appearances and lifestyle at the expense of one's financial health can be as problematic as it can get. The only way out is to understand the root of the problem and acknowledge the issues underneath.

If your money problems are due to your low self-esteem, you need to take it from there and slowly but surely build your self-esteem and self-worth. In Erin Skye Kelly's philosophy of debt, she expressed that human behaviors can be divided into four main areas:

1. Things that might not feel good but are good for us
2. Things that feel good and are good for us
3. Things that feel good but aren't good for us
4. Things that don't feel good and aren't good for us

If many of your habits fall into categories 3 and 4 (a.k.a things that are not good for you such as overspending, accumulating debt, not budgeting, etc.), your self-esteem will just plummet all the more. To improve your belief in yourself, the only way is to make yourself trust 'you' again. To do that, do more of the things that fall under categories 1 and 2. Even if they don't feel good and comfortable, since they are good for you, *choose to do them anyway and commit to them* to rebuild your self-esteem. This will not only benefit how you view yourself, but this also saves you from trouble beyond the financial aspects of your life.

Unprocessed trauma
People with unprocessed trauma may also fall into financial patterns that do not serve them well. Be it divorce, illness, betrayal, failure, or loss, people have different coping mechanisms for unprocessed trauma. One of the usual ways people cope is by shopping or spending more money. Impulsive financial decisions can actually be coping mechanisms to distract you from the actual issue underneath. When you spend more and accumulate new things, you're feeding your brain with a short-lived

high, helping you temporarily forget your emotional burden.

Instead of resorting to these patches or coping mechanisms that are actually causing more harm than good, you first need to identify the trauma in your life, write it down in a journal and ask yourself "What do I need to do to heal?", "Will buying this new item really contribute to my healing?", "How do I confront and process my feelings and past experiences?". There are many other ways to help you heal and process your trauma besides draining your savings and accumulating more debt. You can consider journaling to release your thoughts and emotions; spending time with nature; or seeing a therapist. It's important to unpack your emotional baggage and know the psychological reasons for your money problems to officially start your healing process and steer your life and finances in the right direction. Emotional and financial freedom are amazing gifts that last a lifetime, feel free to give yourself these gifts!

MOST COMMON FINANCIAL MISTAKES

Financial mistakes aren't just about the wrong money decisions you made but also the right financial opportunities you missed. There are all kinds of financial pitfalls many people are stuck with, but the good news is every financial hardship has a way out, and you can always recover from these mistakes by acknowledging them and planning out your next best move. Besides, a mistake is only a mistake if you haven't learned from it. Your financial mistakes are hard-won lessons. Make sure to eke out as much learning as possible from these shortcomings.

We will talk about the most common financial mistakes one by one, and briefly discuss how to address them.

Excessive and frivolous spending
Overspending mistakes have been around since the beginning of money although it's much more challenging to resist the urge to spend these days because of the convenience of online shopping and the abundance

of fun, pretty things we feel we should own. Top that with the army of influencers and the barrage of marketing campaigns swaying you to part with your hard-earned money.

What you should keep in mind is that when you impulsively buy something, you're not actually pursuing an item. You're pursuing a feeling. Retail therapy is named that way because psychologically speaking, it really is therapeutic to shop. Retail therapy is shopping not mainly for necessity's sake but for the sake of cheering yourself up and making yourself feel better. While it can lighten your stress, it can also lighten your wallet, and if left unregulated, it can turn into a more compulsive behavior that can worsen your financial situation.

There are ways to optimize your spending habits without feeling deprived and while still feeling that dose of dopamine shopping brings. First, make it a habit to allocate proper budgeting for your monthly 'wants'. Track your expenses using apps and budgeting tools to avoid overspending. Try to buy only the things that you need and if you do add something to your cart, to minimize impulsive purchases, wait for 30 minutes, hours, or days depending on the item, before you proceed to checkout. If it's an item you don't genuinely want or need, your desire to buy that item is likely to fade or vanish after a few days. Window shopping or browsing shopping sites can actually breed the same feeling as actually shopping because it's simply all about 'anticipating the possibility of a treat'. For a harmless mood booster, try just filling up your online cart and saving the checkout for later to feel good guilt-free.

There will be a whole chapter about budgeting and delayed gratification, and we will talk more about strategies for improving your spending habits.

Never-ending payments

More and more businesses are shifting their structures into the subscription model because it easily translates into recurring revenue and business stability. From grocery to perfume to pest control, you name it, it most likely already has a subscription service model. While this means more convenience on the part of the customers, this also means more monthly expenses that, if unmonitored, could amount to hefty and never-ending payments that could seriously compromise your monthly budget.

If you signed up and subscribed to a lot of products or services, do an inventory on all of them and identify which ones you can forego to ramp up your savings instead. Every dollar counts, so think twice before you sign up for every attractive subscription service you come across.

Living on borrowed money

Sadly, it has become a norm to buy the essentials and pay the bills using credit cards. This can only mean people are spending more than they're making. The thing about borrowing money is that it could become a habit. And unless you pay off your debt right away, the consumer debt will just grow every month, and before you know it, you can no longer keep up with the interest. This doesn't only put you on the losing end, but this could also tremendously harm your credit score. Establish a debt management plan as early as today to avoid piling debt up into an unmanageable number. Be careful spending your hard-earned money, but be extra careful spending money you do not have. This book has an entire chapter on debt management, and we will delve into restoring order in your finances and eventually becoming debt-free.

Buying a new car

Many people trade in their cars every 2-3 years to acquire a new model, paying more interest on a depreciating asset. If you're in this pattern, it means owning a car is no longer just a matter of function in your life but a matter of prestige. It's okay to spend for prestige if you actually have excess money to buy the new car in cash. However, if you are buying it on credit, you're willing to go broke just to look rich. That is a real problem you should prioritize dealing with. Just because you can afford the monthly payments, it doesn't mean you can afford the car. Only a few people actually have enough money to pay for a car in cash. If you don't have savings or you have consumer debt to eliminate, be extra careful with any further expenses and save up every dollar for better opportunities. If your car is still in good condition, perhaps it's best to think about trading it in once you're in a better financial position. And if you do need to buy a new car, it's best to buy one that uses less gas or costs less to maintain and insure.

Spending too much on your house

Your housing costs should ideally not exceed 25% of your monthly income. If you overspend on a house, you're risking foreclosure and a lot of money troubles. There are a lot of other things you can do with your money, so it's important to buy a house that is just enough for your family. The bigger the house, the more expensive the utilities, maintenance, and taxes. To avoid financial stress, be more conservative with your home purchase or rental.

There's actually a term used to refer to people who buy homes beyond their means, sacrificing vacations and discretionary spending. The 'house broke' or 'house poor' may have a large, beautiful home, but they no longer have the means to pursue other personal or financial goals or can no longer afford to think about shifting careers or being flexible with their income source because of their huge default financial obligations. No matter how big your monthly income is, if you spend a chunk of it on housing, you're house poor, and that could get in the way of the lifestyle you're dreaming of.

Using home equity like a piggy bank

Never borrow money against your home. Your home equity is not your piggy bank. If you're thinking about using home equity for unnecessary luxuries, home improvement, and other unnecessary spending, you should definitely think twice. You're risking your shelter which is the main point of your home purchase. You probably will be compelled to use home equity if you encountered unexpected events and didn't have enough emergency savings, but you should really work on your emergency fund to avoid using your home equity as the last resort. You can cash out your equity if you're a retired homeowner who wants to downsize, but for other reasons, consider your decisions carefully before decreasing the equity in your home.

Living paycheck to paycheck

According to a study from Lending Club and PYMNTS, 61% of Americans are living paycheck to paycheck.[36] Even some high-income earners making over $250,000 a year are a part of this statistic. If one missed paycheck will easily cause a financial disaster in your life, it's time to reassess your situation and make a change. To avoid relying on debt for emergencies and survival and avoid being trapped by an endless cycle of toxic debt, it's best to make the decision to take charge of your finances and slowly but surely restore your financial health. This book will discuss in detail how you can do just that.

Not investing in retirement

The best time to start investing in retirement is yesterday. If you still haven't, the time is now. The earlier you start, the more you can capitalize on the power of compounding returns. Social security benefits are not going to be enough to live comfortably after retiring. If you don't want to be a burden to your dependents and want to make the most of the tax benefits of tax-deferred retirement accounts, you should get started with your retirement investments as soon as possible. A whole chapter of this book is all about the best strategies for retirement planning to shape your desired future lifestyle, achieve financial security, and make sound investment decisions today.

Paying off debt with savings

If your debt is accruing 19% interest, and your retirement account is gaining 7%, you may think it makes sense to pay off the high-interest debt using your retirement account, but you need to consider the opportunity cost of compounding returns. Even if you promise to rebuild these accounts as soon as the debt is paid off, the sense of urgency to pay it back usually fades, and if you aren't careful and don't make the necessary changes to your spending habits, you'll end up accumulating debt again, and you'll never be able to recoup your savings and investments. Even disciplined planners find it challenging to set money aside to rebuild retirement accounts after using them up. Should you use your savings to pay off debt, you should honor what you owe to your retirement fund. Otherwise, it's not a good idea to drain your savings to pay off debt. The best move to resolve your debt problem is to either spend less or earn more.

This book covers an entire chapter on how you can establish multiple income streams. Making more money without falling into the trap of lifestyle inflation is key to financial success and freedom.

Not having a plan

What you will have in the future depends on what you decide to do today. You may not be considering a financial plan because you don't have the money to need one anyway. But if you aren't seeing financial progress in your life, it's all the more reason to have a plan and establish your strategy moving forward.

THE REAL WORLD ... Get inspired by the story of Jessica Jabbar, a 27-year-old, career woman from New York City. She's been working in the Big Apple for six years, starting at $6 per hour at her first internship. With consistency and dedication, she's now earning over six figures a month. She's also consistent with her savings goals and sticks to a detailed monthly budget. She hit her $100,000 savings milestone and started to invest while keeping her lifestyle modest and steady to reach even more financial rewards.[37]

A financial plan is mainly about saving, investing, and establishing the right financial goals that are suitable to your exact situation. It's all about effective money management and avoiding financial stress. It's about actively shaping your future to achieve financial stability and peace of mind. With the right plan and willful implementation of the plan, you will soon have the luxury to retire early and live to thrive instead of living to survive.

If you don't know where to start, worry not. I'm here to guide you on all the steps necessary to improve your financial situation and achieve your personal goals. It all starts with the awareness of your financial position, spending habits, and the psychological reasons for your money problems and financial mistakes. Now, it's time to take action.

The journey to financial security is not going to be easy. It will require some sacrifices, focus, and determination. It needs your full commitment and self-discipline. You would need to shift your paradigm and be comfortable choosing to do the things that can serve you well. The journey to financial freedom is exciting and your future self will thank you for it a thousand times over!

- Living on borrowed money
- Buying a new car
- Spending too much on your house
- Using home equity like a piggy bank
- Living paycheck to paycheck
- Not investing in retirement
- Paying off debt with savings
- Not having a financial plan

1. The first step to solving any problem is to acknowledge that there is a problem. Acknowledge the need to improve your financial health and commit to improving your spending habits, managing debt effectively, and working smarter in terms of personal finance.

2. Ask yourself, "How am I holding myself back?" Watch out for self-defeating tendencies that are getting in the way of your financial security. Address the emotional roots of your money problems and find better ways to cope and heal.

EXERCISE

Create a spreadsheet summarizing your **Total Debt** and your **As-Is Budget** to closely examine your financial position.

TOTAL DEBT EXAMPLE

Account	Total Owed	Minimum Monthly
Chase	2,356.00	47.00
American Express	1,860.00	21.00
Car loan	12,500.00	265.00
School loan 1	5,500.00	87.00
School loan 2	12,500.00	165.00

As-Is Budget	Month 1	Month 2	Month 3
Rent			
Utilities			
Vehicle Gas			
Total Debt Payments			
Insurance			
Eat in - Groceries			
Eat out - Restaurants, takeout, delivery			
Personal care			
Savings and Investments			
Subscriptions/			
Memberships			
Miscellaneous expenses			
Total Expenditure			
Total Income			

Chapter 2

PRACTICING SELF-DISCIPLINE & DELAYED GRATIFICATION

As the classic proverb goes, *No pain, no gain.* Self-discipline and delayed gratification may be challenging to grasp, but once mastered, they can lead to financial gains that may translate to your purest form of well-being. The good thing is that these are learnable skills, and through practice, you can harness them to gain more control over your finances, your life, and your future.

THE IMPORTANCE OF SELF-DISCIPLINE

Even if you are the highest-paid personnel in your company, if you cannot regulate your spending habits, you can still drown in debt if you continue to live in excess. Self-discipline will not only help you fare well financially but will also be a core foundation for success in all areas of your life.

Financial discipline is hard to master because people tend to associate spending with happiness. When people start feeling sad or bored, going on a shopping spree usually generates instant gratification to temporarily spike dopamine levels and create feelings of happiness and pleasure. Humans are biologically programmed for instant gratification. The reward system in our brain is naturally there to bolster our survival instinct. Immediate rewards are generally necessary for survival, and our ancestors would prioritize more immediate needs like seeking shelter, finding food, and avoiding threats. However, always resorting to instant gratification could mean loose self-restraint and the inability to make sacrifices for future gain. Instant gratification is all about pursuing and fulfilling 'present' pleasures and gains. It takes work to cultivate the exact opposite which is 'delayed gratification'.

Self-discipline is a key ingredient in order to realize our biggest goals, maximize our resources, avoid self-defeating financial habits, and build financial stability and personal development. With financial discipline, you become more focused and committed to reaching your goals instead of just aimlessly drifting through life. The better you are at following a budget, sacrificing niceties, and regulating your discretionary spending, the faster you can pay down your debt, purchase your dream home, set up your child's college fund, or take that 3-month sabbatical to explore Southeast Asia. Self-discipline can help you lead the life that you want. It can empower all other areas of life, including your career, health and fitness, and even social and relationship goals. It's a catalyst for achieving contentment, happiness, and overall life satisfaction.

Eliminate financial problems through self-discipline

While the lack of self-discipline is not the sole culprit for people's financial problems, it plays a major role in achieving financial well-being. Your ability to adhere to a budget, control impulse buying, save regularly, and make wise financial decisions rely on how self-disciplined you are with your finances.

As mentioned, it's hard to stay disciplined when spending or shopping has an inherent ability to make us instantly happy. Plus, people nowadays have *tremendously easy access to credit (mostly not good!!??)*. Couple that with social media increasing the pressure to show off and the incredibly smart targeting campaigns of retailers online and today's world easily becomes a recipe for financial disaster. With so many temptations to spend money and easy access to seeing other people joyfully succumb to consumerism, it becomes even harder to stay true to your goals and practice this essential skill.

Use self-discipline to rewire your responses about money

For now, in your subconscious mind, 'spending' and 'happiness' are still very much interlinked. However, you can choose to intentionally rewire your responses about money and *connect your 'happiness' wire to saving and investing instead*.

Our responses about money are shaped by various factors including cultural influences, upbringing, and personal experiences. Your current responses about money probably aren't on the healthy side yet. You may still be prone to impulse buying, overspending, procrastinating on your financial goals, and constantly succumbing to instant gratification. However, I encourage you to begin rewiring your thoughts about money in order to find joy and satisfaction in building discipline in your life.

Self-discipline is a powerful driving force to exercise self-restraint and deliberately make healthier financial choices. Rewire your responses about money by first developing *self-awareness* and *the commitment to change*.

Associate happiness with financial independence

You first need to decide how you want to turn your finances around, and you need to actually desire financial health or independence. You can't fool yourself into chasing something that you don't completely want or believe in. You probably would only realize the value of financial security once you start feeling overwhelmed and overburdened by financial problems and constraints. You can either intentionally realize the value of sorting your finances today or wait for life to teach you a lesson as you slowly but surely get yourself into financial hurdles because of the lack of money management and self-discipline.

As soon as you start associating happiness with financial independence, *that's when the magic happens*. All of a sudden, instead of feeling energized when you mindlessly shop and spend, you'll feel guilt instead. Whenever you add more savings into your account, you feel this jolt of energy that is just bound to build that momentum you need to be committed to financial freedom. The more savings you have in your bank account, the more energy it brings and the more you attract money into your life. Make sure to pay yourself first and establish the habit of regularly saving money to collect more energy, happiness, and a sense of pride and hope, knowing that you're finally headed in the right direction.

PRACTICAL TIPS TO FINANCIAL SELF-DISCIPLINE

For a stress-free future, harness your ability to regulate your impulses today. Start by committing to the following healthy financial practices:

Create and stick to a monthly budget

Without a budget, it's easy to mess up your finances. Whether it's using a spreadsheet or a budgeting app, make sure you keep track of your expenses and stick to a budget to avoid overspending. In the next chapter, we will be exploring budget creation. For now, review this book's Chapter 1 Exercise about your As-Is Budget and perhaps calculate some averages for the monthly spending in each category. Awareness of your current state will help you create a realistic budget, which we will discuss further in the next chapter.

A budget is a foundational tool for financial discipline. Setting spending limits is the best way to keep financial stability and avoid accumulating debt. Budgeting also enables you to allocate funds properly, secure your savings, and take real strides towards the joy of financial freedom.

By tracking your expenses, you can also get a clearer understanding of your spending patterns and identify which areas you can improve on. Budgeting may be a basic solution, but it's the very core of building a better financial future.

Pay off your credit card debt in full every month

There's nothing wrong with preferring to pay on credit instead of cash as long as you don't allow interest charges to accrue and go out of hand. Paying off your credit card debt in full every month not only helps you ditch the interest charges but also allows you to make the most of credit card rewards. With easy apps on our smartphones, you can even make quick payments to help defray the monthly bill. You could even make a $5 payment to a credit card whenever you skip the fancy coffee or the dessert you are too full for anyway! In addition, your credit card should pay at least 2% cashback on ALL purchases. If it doesn't, it's best to switch to one that does.

Carrying a credit card balance from month to month can also increase your credit utilization rate which can negatively affect your credit score and loan applications. Most importantly, not paying off your credit card debt sooner can cause you to get stuck in a debt cycle and puts you in an avoidable financial strain. Take note that most credit card interest is compounded daily. You'll then be *paying interest on your interest*, and as you continue to incur more compounded interest, your debt will only grow and spiral out of control.

Have the self-discipline to prevent such unnecessary and unwanted trouble and make it a habit to settle your credit card bill *in full every month*. It may take several months to get there, but once you do, enjoy the freedom and never let go!

Open a high-yield savings account and save a set amount every month

You can start saving whatever amount. The key is to just get started with the habit of saving consistently. It can even be as low as $20 per month, and it will add up over time! In addition to being able to actually save something, you'll also slowly but surely build your trust and confidence in your own ability to stick to healthy financial habits and take charge of your finances.

Pay yourself first and consider saving as another monthly bill instead of an optional allocation. Some high-yield savings accounts are at a 2% interest rate. While the returns may not be as substantial as what you get from investing, you can just consider saving in a high-yield interest account as your emergency fund. If you haven't secured an emergency fund yet, it's high time that you do. It generates peace of mind knowing that you have a savings account to dip into should emergencies come up. To build your emergency fund, aim to save at least 3-6 months' worth of living expenses. This way, should unforeseen events like sudden unemployment crop up, you still have the buffer to move on with life without being financially distressed.

Set your financial goals

Setting financial goals is important to actually shape life the way you want it instead of just drifting aimlessly. Your financial goals should follow the SMART formula:

Specific—What needs to be accomplished?

Measurable—How do you know you achieved the goal? What number or exact scenario are we talking about?

Attainable—Is the goal (as well as the deadline) really doable or realistic?

Relevant—Is the goal in line with your values and priorities?

Time-bound—When should you achieve the goal?

You can't achieve the most tangible manifestation of your goals, dreams, and aspirations without proper goal-setting and planning. The first step to realizing your financial goals is to set them, so be very clear about how much you want and when you want it. That way, you can break it up into smaller chunks and know exactly how much to save up every month to meet your target number and deadline.

You can also set short-term, mid-term, and long-term goals. You can consider your long-term goals as your prime or top goals and you can set the short and medium-term goals as stepping stones to achieve your main goals.

Short-term goals

Short-term goals can generally be achieved within a year. They're actionable, so you can do them now or soon. Examples of short-term goals include:

- Saving up the same amount every month for your emergency fund
- Creating a budget and sticking to it for 6 months
- Saving up $200 a month for 8 months for a home improvement project
- Paying off a credit card debt of $1000
- Saving up for a $500-weekend excursion

Mid-term goals

Medium-term goals can be achieved in 1-5 years. Setting mid-term goals can help you move even closer to your long-term aspirations. Achieving your mid-term goals can generate a strong sense of accomplishment and are big wins you should savor and celebrate. Examples of mid-term goals include:

- Securing your 6-month emergency fund
- Paying off all high-interest debt
- Saving for education
- Saving for a major purchase like a car, furniture, high-tech gadget, etc.
- Securing capital to start your own business

Long-term goals

Long-term goals are the bigger ones that would take at least 5 years to achieve. Examples include:

- Building your retirement savings
- Becoming completely debt-free
- Owning a property
- Achieving financial independence

Stay focused on your financial goals

Setting a financial goal is the easy part. Staying focused and committed to achieving them is the hardest bit. The best way to stay committed to your goals is to make sure that you set goals closest to your heart, those that match your personal values and priorities.

For example, if you've been constantly stressed financially and you're just plain sick of it, you are most likely going to be more motivated to religiously stick to your budget and savings plan. If you badly want to buy your dream home and have your very own space, you are more inclined to delay gratification to finally become a homeowner. If you hate working so much and want to spend the rest of your life traveling, relaxing, volunteering or doing work that is most meaningful to you, you are bound to crave financial freedom and early retirement more intensely. Your goals are a reflection of who you want to be and how you want to live your life in line with your core values and identity.

Find your deepest why and know your deepest desires and allow yourself to drown in them. Stay focused and hang in there. As long as you're willing to make sacrifices today to reap bigger rewards in the future, you will soon live the life you've always imagined.

One powerful way to help you stay focused on your financial goals is visualization. Envisioning the end result and looking at your roadmap strengthens your emotional connection to your goals. You can put up a picture of one of your short, medium, and long-term goals somewhere in your home that you can see every day. A short term goal might be to buy the newest iPhone, so put a picture of it up on your bathroom mirror. Plan on saving $25/month towards this goal and skip the $5 coffee occasionally and put it towards this goal. A long term goal might be to go on a cruise. Again, put a picture up somewhere in your space (or work desk) and make a savings plan. You can also establish a system where you get to check and visualize your finances on a daily basis. It could be in the form of pie charts, spreadsheets, budgeting apps, or just checking your bank account and CC balances every day.

Determine your needs vs. your wants
It goes without saying that your needs are the expenses you can't live without including food, utilities, rent, transportation costs, clothing, etc. Your wants are expenses you can comfortably live without; they aren't crucial for your survival. Going to movies, eating out, and buying random things are some common 'wants' that you should regulate if you want to get serious about achieving financial security. Review the exercise from Chapter 1 and calculate the percentage of your monthly expenditures that fall under "wants." Awareness of your current position and how you could trim things in a relatively painless way is a good place to start.

When it comes to budgeting, you can follow the 50/30/20 rule. 50% of your income for your needs; 30% for your wants; and 20% for your savings. This is just an example and not necessarily hard-set. The exact formula depends on your income and expenses. For example, if you bought a house you can barely afford, the proportion can be totally different. Though, it is ideal to make the necessary adjustments to live below your means and cut back on your basic expenses in such a way that they would only take up 50% of your income.

Saving and investing can also be considered 'needs' because they are necessary for your future goals and well-being. Retirement funds, paying off debt, life insurance, and other financial goals can be considered 'needs' and should be treated as such.

Reduce, reuse, recycle

This may not sound like a grand piece of advice, but it's one that makes sense and is a great habit to adopt in your home and in your lifestyle at large.

Instead of readily spending money on items that are just 'wants', you can get creative by considering reducing, reusing, or recycling items first. For example, you can sell items you no longer need or perhaps launch a garage sale to have funds for buying potential wants. Or perhaps you already have a similar item at home that you can use or repurpose instead of acquiring a new one. Women spend an average of $100-$400 per month on new clothing, and packing their wardrobes with piles of clothes month in and month out can lead to a lot of redundancy and impulse purchases, not to mention clutter. In terms of clothing, it's best to go for more classic pieces and colors and those that you can imagine wearing multiple times. Most likely, if you clean your wardrobe, you would find items that feel brand new because of how long it has been since the last time you saw them!

Avoid peer pressure to spend

It can't be helped to spend whenever you hang out with friends, and giving up your social life just to save more can also be limiting and technically not healthy. The best way to get the best of both worlds is to create a budget for these events and stick to it. If you are almost running out of budget, perhaps instead of buying 2-3 drinks, just go for one. Instead of a movie night, go for a matinee. All the little adjustments count. And perhaps instead of befriending just anyone, focus on quality instead of quantity in your social circle. Keep the real friendships and do away with the shallow ones. It's not only about saving money in the process. It's also about allocating your time and energy to things and people that actually matter.

WHAT IS DELAYED GRATIFICATION?

We live in a world where everything is made faster, easier, and more convenient. With express food and grocery deliveries; easy access to entertainment; and the convenience of credit cards, we can have everything we want and need in no time. While modern society has made things simpler and more convenient, we can't deny the fact that exposing ourselves to instant gratification day in and day out is making it harder for us to stay patient in terms of strategizing long-term goals.

Delayed gratification is all about trading short-term pleasure for long-term gain. According to Sigmund Freud's "pleasure principle", we humans are wired to chase pleasure and avoid pain. Opting for instant gratification is our very nature. However, as we mature, the "reality principle" kicks in, and we start considering risks versus rewards, giving us the ability to delay immediate pleasure to gain greater rewards later on. The ability to delay gratification is a learned behavior, and it's a crucial skill to master in terms of achieving financial freedom and stability.

A major component of delaying gratification is **impulse control**. It's all about *'thinking before acting'*. However, managing impulses is easier said than done. Good thing there are impulse control strategies you can adopt to slowly but surely get better at regulating your impulses. For example, you can choose to delay or slow down your reaction time. Instead of proceeding to checkout immediately after browsing an online shop, give it 24 hours to finalize your decision. The same way when regulating the impulse to immediately react after being aggravated. Allowing some time before you react can help you keep cool and adopt more logical and composed responses. Being able to control impulse gratification is a crucial life skill that can help you avoid bad decisions and choose the things that are most beneficial for your future and for your well-being.

To fully internalize this concept, take a moment to reflect on that exact situation in the past when you acted or splurged on impulse. Perhaps you made a huge purchase that you regretted after a day or two.

Perhaps you allowed your emotions to get the better of you and you have painfully hurt someone you loved. Thinking before acting can save you a lot of trouble in all aspects of life.

Long-term thinking is another key component of mastering delayed gratification. Being able to question and intentionally shape our choices and decisions today to build a better future is at the core of delayed gratification. Just like what Amazon CEO Jeff Bezos highlights in his letter to Amazon shareholders from 1997, "We can't realize our potential as people or as companies unless we plan for the long term".

It might take just around 30 days to create a habit, but that change in habit could potentially transform your life for the next 30 years. It'll just take around an hour to complete a workout, but that workout session can set your mood *for the next 12 hours*. It might take 3-6 months to learn a new skill, but that skill can make you millions if you play the game right. Long-term thinking is not just a lofty ideal; it has the power to positively (or negatively) impact the rest of your life.

While they're not the easiest skills to master, impulse control, long-term thinking, and delayed gratification are all keys to building wealth, achieving financial freedom, and pursuing your best life. You can do it!

The following are some examples of delayed gratification at play:

- **Relationships**
  Choosing to put your phone down and resisting the urge to succumb to the instant gratification of social media in order to be fully present with your loved one.

- **Career**
  Resisting the temptation to binge-watch on Netflix or scroll through social media for hours to use your free time more productively in learning new knowledge and skills to advance your career.

- **Health**
  Choosing to decline the instant gratification of eating chocolate cake to reap better and healthier rewards of more energy and vitality.

- **Finances**
Resisting to buy things you don't absolutely need to enjoy the long-term rewards of more savings and financial independence.

   However, if you are used to spending money as soon as you get it, it would take more willpower and effort to change the way you handle your finances. That is why in the next sections, I'm going to walk you through some actionable tips that can help you reap the incredible benefits of mastering delayed gratification.

Delayed gratification is key to wealth

The ability to delay gratification is a major predictor of success. Forty years of Stanford Research found that people who can delay gratification are more likely to succeed. It's also known as the **Marshmallow Experiment**, with children as respondents.

Each child is brought into a private room and sat down in a chair with one marshmallow on the table in front of them. They were offered a deal. The researcher told them that he was going to leave the room and if the child didn't eat the marshmallow while the researcher was away, he would be rewarded with a second marshmallow, but if he eats it before the researcher came back, there will be no second marshmallow.

It's the classic representation of delayed gratification– either one treat today or more treats later.

As the years passed, the children grew up, and the researchers made follow-up studies. Indeed, the children who chose to delay gratification and get the second marshmallow ended up getting higher SAT scores, lower chances of obesity, lower levels of substance abuse, better stress responses, and better social skills. The researchers followed the development of the same group of children for 40 years, and the results were consistent. *This only goes to show how powerful delayed gratification can indeed be.*

Delayed gratification leads to better outcomes

Delayed gratification can empower not just the financial aspects of your life. It can also lead to better outcomes in all areas of life including health and fitness, academic achievement, relationships, and personal development. Delayed gratification is rooted in your ability to make the best decisions today to positively shape your future circumstances. It's about understanding that the little sacrifices you make today can pay huge dividends in the future.

Delayed gratification is something you can learn

You don't have to learn and master it overnight. Just take baby steps and work your way up gradually. You can start with simple yet crucial things like setting spending limits, creating a monthly budget and sticking to it, or simply shopping with a list. All the little things will add up, and before you know it, it's already embedded into your system and being mindful of your financial decisions already becomes more second nature to you.

Trust that the reward is coming

The world is governed by many laws including the "Law of Sowing and Reaping", also known as the Law of Cause and Effect or the Law of Karma. The law states that every action we take has a corresponding consequence or outcome. It illustrates that positive actions are bound to lead to positive outcomes, and negative actions will often lead to negative consequences. If you choose to follow positive habits and good decision-making, the results or output is bound to match your input. Trust that, even though your efforts will not lead to instant results, they will and shall bring about the big rewards you so desire and deserve.

Know exactly how long you have to wait

The best way to keep your focus and motivation is to set a timeline for your goals and take an appropriate course of action. By being strategic about your financial and personal goals and calculating your input in such a way that you can meet your target deadlines, you will be more motivated to stick to your habits and routine to achieve your goals in due time.

Distract yourself in the meantime

It can be hard to stick to a monthly budget or save for the future when it's so easy and exhilarating to shop and spend. If you are working towards a long-term goal that compels you to delay gratification for longer, in order to avoid going astray, you can think about having a go-to list of activities or distractions when your urge to spend or give in is strong. There could be a lot of things that you do enjoy doing. Perhaps you can temporarily go for the hobbies, activities, or distractions that won't necessitate too much spending.

For example:

- watching a good movie;
- reading a good e-book;
- going for a run;
- pampering yourself with a luxurious homemade bubble bath;
- or whatever it is that can lift your mood without spending a lot.

Choose the second marshmallow

Just like in the Stanford Marshmallow experiment, choose to be a bit more patient and wait for the bigger reward that can lay the tracks for your future success. Patience and self-regulation are key. Your ability to delay gratification can definitely dictate how your future unfolds and whether or not you get to live the life you truly want.

HOW TO DELAY GRATIFICATION

How do you exercise restraint? How do you deliberately avoid all temptations that could compromise your future? According to the Federal Reserve, the average US household owed $7,123 on credit cards. For Americans, it's normal to use dollars they don't have in order to pay for current expenses. Some of these expenses are not even necessary. Some pay for luxury with borrowed money. This only reflects how delayed gratification is a huge challenge across the country, and in actuality, across the developed world.

It's not just about self-control

The inability to delay gratification is not 100% about the lack of self-control. While it could be one of the factors, there are other influences we should take into account. Everyone has their own story, and everyone is in different places in life. For people who haven't found their clearest goal yet or those who just can't find the motivation and are still a bit lost in life, their primary goal is probably to pick themselves up again and restore their life force. There are also environmental factors at play such as upbringing, socio-economic status, and toxic environments that disable them from realizing their best potential. In short, the pursuit of mastering delayed gratification is mainly for those who are ready for the challenge, who are determined, and who have found their motivation to turn their life around. For the rest of the population, there are other deeper and more crucial underlying issues to take care of, but sooner or later, when the time is right for them, they will also feel the need to start this journey.

Ways to delay gratification

If you are one of those folks who are still struggling with delaying gratification, here are some of the strategies that may prove to be helpful.

Out of sight, out of mind

This avoidance technique is simple yet powerful. Sometimes, the best way to avoid temptation is to get rid of it.

- On a diet? Stop buying junk and stocking up your pantry with unhealthy snacks.
- Want to eliminate debt? Minimize adding more debt by ditching credit cards. Start paying in cash from here on out.
- Want to avoid getting distracted or constantly shopping online? Delete the apps or keep your phone hidden away from your desk, perhaps in the farthest room in the house.

There are many ways to trick our brains, and most of the time, they work.

Remind yourself of what you're giving up

When you give up mindless shopping and impulse buying, it may be easy to think that you're giving up happiness and stress relief. But if you really think about it, what you're giving up is actually the financial strain of accumulating unnecessary things, the clutter that mindless shopping leads to, and the toxic habit that can cause you more trouble than it's worth.

The next time you find it hard to resist instant gratification, ask yourself "What am I really giving up here?" Remind yourself that you're doing this ultimately for your well-being and for a more stress-free life. A simple practice to drive this home would be to *spend 30 minutes cleaning out one area of clutter in your home.* I bet you will discover some things you bought that you were really excited about at that time, but look where they ended up– forgotten, unused, and under a pile of old shoes!

Have realistic, time-bound goals

It's important to have a target to focus on. Without clarity and time frame, it can be easy to slack off and slip into the same old, unhealthy patterns. Having time-bound and realistic goals also makes it easy to measure progress and stay committed to what you have resolved to do.

It's easy to procrastinate when goals are loose and vague. As you break down your long-term goals into smaller, more manageable milestones and as you attach time frames to each milestone, make sure to celebrate small wins along the way and pat yourself on the back for having made progress in your quest for personal development and financial freedom. Perhaps you can treat yourself to a nice staycation after securing your emergency fund. Or it could be as simple as taking a break, enjoying an afternoon latte, or pampering yourself with a hot bath or a hot workout for the small wins and progress that you make every day.

Learn to work with your emotions, not against them

Mark Manson contends that the best way to successfully harness self-discipline is not denying emotions but accepting them. Forcing yourself to delay gratification is not sustainable. You will easily lose motivation if your pursuit is backed by self-denial. Creatively finding ways to enjoy your pursuit or finding ways to hate the consequence of going astray is the more sustainable route. Perhaps for now spending money is your idea of 'feeling good'. You can't simply force yourself to think that spending doesn't feel good. You have to associate 'feeling good' with something else that supports your goal.

Mark Manson also emphasizes how it's important to start the journey coming from a place of self-acceptance instead of self-loathing. If you're pursuing this journey because you feel shame and guilt over your past mistakes and poor decisions, that's not the best way to start. Avoid overgeneralizing and learn to separate mistakes from your self-worth and identity. Just because you did something bad, it doesn't necessarily mean you're a bad person as a whole. Feeling bad about something is simply a reminder that there's something in your life that you need to pay attention to. It doesn't define your entirety as a human being.

The best way to successfully form a habit, practice self-discipline, or pursue any goal is to start with self-compassion and self-acceptance. If you're doing the right things because you love yourself and you genuinely care about your own well-being, it's easier to be motivated to do the right things. Instead of being driven by self-loathing, be fueled by self-regard. That alone can make a huge difference in how you start and continue your journey.

Hang out with the right people

It would be hard to practice delayed gratification if you're surrounded by people who tend to overspend and overindulge. In life, it's either you 'influence' or 'be influenced'. If you think that you can do just fine sticking to your goals despite your social circle pulling you in different directions, then perhaps you don't need to make a change.

However, if you think that your existing circle does not align with the goals you have set for yourself and you can't stand or resist their negative influence, consider finding a better environment that shows support, encouragement, accountability, and positive influence. Jim Rohn says "You are the average of the five people you spend the most time with", and while it's not easy to switch friends, you are the only one who can tell what your best move should be.

CONCLUSION

To execute on this chapter takes a lot of patience, discipline, and even self-reflection. As you try out different strategies to keep yourself focused and motivated, it would also take a lot of trial and error, and in the process, it opens the door to self-discovery. You don't figure out everything as soon as you decide to figure it all out! That's not how it works. You figure life out slowly but surely, little by little, and before you know it, you realize how far you've come and how all the little sacrifices and delayed gratification are actually worth it.

THE REAL WORLD ... Let the story of Terry Carter inspire you. He was barely getting by after graduating from law school. He and his best friend decided to be serious about delaying gratification and setting budget goals. They would call each other to rationalize big expenses, and after just three years of saving consistently, Terry had enough money for a condo down payment. With the habit of delaying gratification ingrained in him, he's now the CEO of Travertine Spa, and he can only imagine bigger things ahead.[37]

4 FINANCIAL MISTAKES TO AVOID

- Not sticking to a monthly budget
- Not paying off credit card debt in full every month
- Not starting a savings account and savings plan
- Not having a financial goal

KEY TAKEAWAYS

1. Self-discipline is a tool that helps you create a lifestyle that supports your financial and personal goals.

2. Delayed gratification is all about trading short-term pleasure for long-term gain. Impulse control and long-term thinking are necessary to successfully resist the urge for instant gratification.

3. Before you start your journey to mastering delayed gratification, make sure that you are coming from a place of self-compassion and self-regard. Don't beat yourself up, but rather, make this journey all about self-improvement and healthy, sustainable progress.

EXERCISE

Put self-discipline into practice by doing this habit-tracking exercise!

Let's do the 60-day challenge! Secure a mini desk calendar, and choose a financial habit you want to form. Put a check on your calendar each day that you have acted successfully to overcome a habit that has been putting a strain on your finances. Choose at least one of the challenges below.

- Ditch buying coffee outside and brew your own at home.

- Stop using credit cards and start paying in cash

- Create a monthly budget and stick to it

- Save at least $5 per day in your piggy bank or money jar

- Practice the 24-hour rule whenever you feel like buying something.

Chapter 3

CREATING A GUILT-FREE BUDGET

Whenever you spend money on yourself, you often end up paying interest—not necessarily in money, but in guilt.

We have all experienced feeling guilt whenever we swipe our credit card at a store. A wave of both excitement and guilt hits us, and we somehow find it hard to draw the line between rewarding and restricting ourselves. That is *guilt-filled spending*, and the only way to go about it is to create a *guilt-free budget*.

Whenever you feel guilty about spending, it actually comes from a place of *awareness*. You are *aware* that you're sacrificing your goals, or you are *aware* that you're spending outside of your budget. Whether you regret a purchase or actually loved it but are just guilty over the dent it made in your pocket, just remember that it doesn't have to be that way. You have the right, and soon will have the ability, to spend guilt-free without compromising your financial goals!

The key is to make room for *'fun money'* in your monthly budget. Not having money allocated for self-care or fun can just do more harm than good. Too much restriction can only lead to overspending. Also, restrictions can create a poor money mindset or *scarcity mindset*, so make sure to factor fun and self-care into your budget, and spend it guilt-free. Just be sure to stick to that allocated budget and spend it on things that matter to you, things that truly make you feel recharged.

For example, my 25-year-old daughter and her husband are fond of traveling. One time, they went to Jamaica on a vacation with her cousin and her husband. My daughter saved up for about 10 months to pay for that trip. Meanwhile, her cousin paid for that trip on credit. My daughter was able to enjoy their vacation with more peace of mind knowing that they'd already paid for it and created no debt. Her cousin and husband paid for that vacation plus interest for a full year after the trip. My daughter made money in interest as she saved, her cousin paid interest after the fact. My daughter hates debt, and for her, every time she's paying through cash, she's essentially saving money by ditching interest. That mindset allowed her to organize her finances extremely efficiently at a relatively young age (25).

Budgeting your fun money may involve doing trade-offs though. In order to build the vacation money, you may need to cut back on going out to dinner or shopping for more clothes. However, you can freely decide how you want to allocate your funds. Just set it according to your priorities and what you value. Tell me how you spend your money and I'll tell you what your priorities are. Your idea of fun could be home decor, new shoes, a new tennis racket or weight belt. It's something totally personal to you, and as long as you plan it in your budget, you can spend your fun money 100% guilt-free. In fact, it's even better than guilt-free, you experience *greater* satisfaction, and even *joy* in the purchase because through it, you are actually contributing to your financial freedom. Wow!

WHY BUDGET?

As you stick to your budget allocations and follow a monthly budget, you concretely work towards your long-term goals *and* avoid drowning in debt.

If you don't create a budget and plan your finances, and you end up randomly tossing your money at every shiny, new object that catches your eye, how will you be able to save up for a house down payment or pay off your debt?

Reasons why you need a budget
If you tend to associate budgeting with restrictions, and you need more convincing as to why you should take this balancing act seriously, let's go over some of the biggest reasons why budgeting is the smartest step to take.

1. **It helps you keep an eye on the prize.** Whatever end goal you have in mind, be it saving for a down payment on a house, starting a business, paying off debt, or planning for retirement, *budgeting is your most basic and essential tool to ensure that you're on the right track*. It's hard to keep your finances in check without following a budget, and if you have a specific destination and timeline you want for yourself, failing to adhere to a budget is the easiest way to mess it all up. *Keep your eye on the prize and hang in there.* It's going to be worth it and the more you stay patient and delay gratification, the sooner you'll enjoy the biggest outcomes.

2. **It helps ensure you don't spend money you don't have.** Credit cards have made it so easy for people to spend money they don't have. The average credit card debt per household in the US is $5,733 as per a 2023 report by TransUnion[3]. People tend to abuse and overuse credit cards to the point of overspending and drowning in debt. Creating and sticking to a budget is one of the easiest ways to avoid putting yourself in this position. By knowing how much money you actually have, how much you can afford to spend, and how much you should save, you become more in control of your finances and avoid destructive financial habits that will only hold you back.

3. **It sets you up for a happier retirement—maybe even early retirement!** Since you are living within your means and paying yourself first, you get to save more and regularly set aside a part of your monthly earnings to your IRA, 401(k), or other retirement instruments. By making little sacrifices today, you are bound to enjoy a happy, stress-free retirement, and depending on your goals, you can even aim for early retirement to have more time and freedom to do what matters the most to you in this lifetime.

4. **It helps you prepare for emergencies.** Anything can happen in life. Our homes will need costly unexpected repairs from time to time. We could get sick or injured or perhaps get laid off or go through a divorce. Since life could be a series of surprises that can lead to financial turmoil, it's best to secure an emergency fund to become better prepared. Your emergency fund should be at least 3-6 months' worth of monthly expenses, and if you don't have an emergency fund yet, make sure to include saving up for it in your next budgeting plan.

5. **It helps shed light on bad spending habits.** It's easy to be aware of your spending habits if you can examine them closely. As you view your expenses, you may notice lots of things you don't really need like a cable TV subscription or daily trips to Starbucks. You can then see which parts you can cut back on and which ones you can further optimize to speed up reaching your financial goals.

6. **It's better than counting sheep.** Have you ever tossed and turned at night worrying about how you can pay your bills and get by? It's easy to get anxious when you're dealing with something unknown. If your financial situation is unknown to you, the best way to gain clarity is to create and stick to a budget. That way, you'll never lose sleep over financial worries again! Nothing feels

better than choosing to be in control of your own life and carving your own path to financial freedom. Believe it or not, financial freedom significantly impacts psychological and emotional freedom and overall contentment in life.

STARTING EARLY

The earlier you understand the key principles of personal finance, the sooner you can make progress and sharpen your mindset, decision-making, and attitude towards financial security.

Why you should start budgeting in your 20's
Younger generations may find it challenging to pursue their financial goals with student loan debt and rising inflation rates weighing them down. In an era where living paycheck to paycheck is the norm, you may feel like the cards are stacked against you.

However, no matter how small or big your paycheck is, with budgeting and delayed gratification, saving money is still **always** possible. *It doesn't matter how little you save.* What matters is forming the habit of saving money and being consistent about keeping your financial health in order. *Once you start saving, it literally snowballs!* I have this friend who asserted that he could not even set aside $20/month for savings, and yet he was an avid smoker and drinker. He earned well over $2000/month and felt that saving even 1% was beyond his ability. Until he realizes the importance of budgeting, saving money will remain an impossibility for him. Budgeting has the power to set him free and help him live a better life.

There are a lot of advantages to starting to budget, save, and invest, especially in your 20's. Let's explore all the benefits one by one.

Saving early means earning more out of every dollar
The earlier you start, the more you get to earn later on. You can always count on the *power of compound interest*. Investing your money early

means you don't just earn interest on your money but eventually *earn interest on your interest*! The more time you allow it to grow, the more you can earn out of every dollar invested.

The same way that compound interest can work wonders when you save and invest, compound interest can also wreak havoc if you fail to budget and resort to debt. Let's revisit the Jamaican trip example of my daughter and her cousin.

If my daughter did not save up for the trip and went on that vacation on credit just like her cousin, the compound interest incurred would've looked like this:

If it was a $3000 trip for the couple, and it took 10 months to pay off the debt at an APR of 17%, the debt plus interest would amount to $3492 in 10 months. The total interest incurred would have been $492, which could've been put away as savings if the couple just chose to budget and save up for the trip instead of vacationing on borrowed money. My daughter saved $492 by ditching debt and relying on the power of simple budgeting. In addition, she earned $30 in interest as she saved!!!

Budgeting prepares you for future "adulting"
For now, home ownership might not be on your mind yet, but you are bound to think about it down the line. Following a budget is the foundation of good money management, which is critical in your 'adulting' phase. The future may seem overwhelming or intimidating as you expect more responsibilities and expenses. However, you don't have to do something grand to do 'adulting' right. Something as simple as 'budgeting' is already the constant you need to set yourself in the right financial direction.

Take the example of two high school graduates who worked full-time at Walgreens for 6 months while taking classes at the local community college. They then purchased a home and rented it out. Within 3 months, they purchased their second rental home and in less than a year after graduating from high school, they are already successful - and profitable - landlords. Set goals and dream big people! It's never too early to start working your way to financial freedom.

Afford the lifestyle you want
A spending plan allows you to actively shape your desired lifestyle. Instead of wasting money on random purchases, having a budget allows you to be strategic about spending money only *on the things that support the lifestyle you want.* If traveling matters the most to you, perhaps you can cut back on buying a $6 latte whenever you pass by that coffee shop near work.

Go debt-free faster
Being debt-free is probably one of the most liberating achievements in your adulthood. Routinely saving a fixed amount every month for the sole purpose of debt elimination is a simple *yet empowering* act. The sooner you can be debt-free, the sooner you can eliminate that dreaded debt anxiety and focus on the next big things life has in store for you.

Less stress when dealing with unplanned expenses
We talked about emergency funds, and harnessing a spending plan to take care of unplanned expenses is just something that can't be understated. From emergency dental appointments to leaks in your roof, life just happens and you know it (remember that fender bender last summer?). Instead of feeling stressed when such surprises crop up, having an emergency fund you can dip into allows you to move forward with life with less stress and more grace. If not, you would end up resorting to high-interest loans or groveling to your parents or friends to save the day (go ahead and raise your hand if you can relate to this).

BUDGETING 101: HOW TO BUDGET MONEY

A budget is simply a plan where you decide how you will spend your income every month. *It's one of the key foundations of financial planning.* It shows two main things (a) how much money you make and (b) how you spend your money. With budgeting, you can see where your money is going from month to month.

You may find it restricting and laborious, but it's actually designed to help you understand and assess your relationship with money. Budgeting is a tool to help you reach your personal and financial goals. It also bolsters a positive relationship with money *and brings a freedom hitherto unknown* - you can trust me on this, or just dive in and experience it for yourself!

Understanding the budgeting process

In the next few pages, we will talk about some of the budgeting methods you can use to organize your finances better. However, do remember that it takes trial and error to find the process that works for you. Aim to find and create a process that meets your needs, desires, and goals *and gets your blood pumping for the project.* The truth is, *if you don't love it, you won't do it.* So let's find a budget you love!

How to budget money

The question is how do you get started? If you have not mastered the habit and skill of budgeting, what is the foolproof approach to follow? Let's look into the process step by step:

1. **Figure out your monthly income.** The first step is to determine your monthly take-home pay after taxes. If you are a freelancer or have a small business, your income may naturally fluctuate. To determine your take-home pay, just get the average of 6-12 months of your income. Looking back at the Chapter 1 Exercise will give you a leg up here.

2. **Track and categorize average monthly spending.** The next key step is to track and organize your total monthly expenses. From basic utilities to other expenses, just gather all data to identify your current spending situation. You can break the expenses down into categories like living expenses, groceries, subscriptions, transportation, debt payments, entertainment, etc. This way, you can know which areas you can regulate in order to save more money. This would be a good time to expand that Chapter 1 exercise to 3 months.

3. **Set a goal and adjust your spending to stay on budget.** If your goal is to first build your emergency fund, determine when you want to achieve that goal and calculate how much you need to save per month to achieve the target amount and deadline. Once you set a goal like this, you need to factor this new goal into your budget and make the necessary adjustments to other expenses to accommodate the more worthwhile goal. Then make a commitment by *scheduling an automatic transfer to savings 2 or 3 days after each payday*. This gives you skin in the game.

    For example, if you used to spend $200 per month on clothes, perhaps you can reduce it to $150 to save the rest for your emergency fund. Evaluate your list of expenses and adjust according to what makes sense and what's doable for you. It will require delaying gratification and making trade-offs, but once you set and achieve your financial goals, it will bolster your confidence and discipline and propel you to achieving bigger financial milestones down the road.

4. **Review your budget regularly.** As you take on more commitments and responsibilities and as you move to the next things life has in store for you, your income and expenses may change, and that makes it important to revisit your budget and check to see

if it can support the new changes in your lifestyle, obligations, or priorities. The budget that worked for you last year may no longer work for you this year, and that's OK.

When creating, evaluating, or reshaping a budget, it's important to keep it sustainable by being realistic and finding a framework that actually works for you. *Tweak as often as you need to until you find the exact method that meets your current needs.*

BUDGETING METHODS

To give you an idea of how to establish your budgeting framework, I will share some of the effective budgeting methods you can apply to your own personal finances. Let's carefully go over the common budgeting methods in personal finance.

The 50-30-20 budgeting method
With this method, all you have to do is divide your budget into three categories:

> 50% - **Needs** (Housing, utilities, groceries, health insurance, car payment)
> 30% - **Wants** (Shopping, hobbies, travel, entertainment, eating out)
> 20% - **Savings** (Savings, debt payments, investments)

Setting aside 30% of your income for wants gives you the freedom to spend that budget allocation however you want, helping you spend on things you love guilt-free.
Good for:

- Beginners who want a simpler approach to budgeting
- Those who need more flexibility in their budget plan

The envelope method

This is a more old-school approach, but many people still prefer it because it allows for stricter spending limits and eliminates their reliance on credit cards. Spending in cash and ditching credit cards further reduce the chances of impulse buying and mindless spending. This method, as the name suggests, literally involves using dedicated envelopes for every spending category.

Good for:

- People who prefer using cash instead of credit card
- Those who need to regulate their reliance on credit cards and establish better financial boundaries.

Bullet journals

Bullet journals are personalized log books organized and updated regularly. It's a finance tracker that you can customize to your liking. If you don't want to make it from scratch, you can find budget journal printables and templates online that you can download and use. It's more like your finance diary, and you can format it however you like. You can track expenses, savings goals, and debt repayment or use it as a regular journal for financial reflections.

Good for:

- Those who like to physically write down their plans
- People who are visual learners and are creative in nature

CONCLUSION

When it comes to budgeting, *there is no right or wrong way.* Everyone who decides to follow a budget prefers different methods but shares a common goal. Budgeting is all about healthy regulations in terms of spending, and the best way to do that is to focus on *value-based spending*. That entails spending on what fuels you. Try to ask yourself these questions:

- What makes you happy?
- What are the things you want to experience?
- What are the things that excite you?
- What kind of change do you want to happen in your financial life?
- What drains your joy and energy?

In Marie Kondo's words, focus on things that "spark joy". Generally speaking, accumulate only the things, activities, and relationships that bring you genuine happiness. When it comes to personal finance, since you don't have unlimited funds, make sure to spend your hard-earned discretionary income on things that support your happiness and well-being. Our priorities and the things that we value vary. Only you know what truly matters to you. Instead of spending according to impulse, intentionally spend on the things that fuel your life and bring you joy. Giving yourself permission to spend and indulge by allocating a budget for fun and self-care and intentionally spending on things that matter to you are the core foundations of a **guilt-free budget**.

THE REAL WORLD . . . Take it from the story of Camilo Maldonado. Growing up poor, he has never learned how to handle finances at home. When he went to college, he had to stretch his dollars and get a grip of his financial situation to get by. He used to spend money in all areas– travel, entertainment, restaurants, etc. Then he started having serious money problems, he realized that if he doesn't track where his money's going, he could never bring order to chaos. He started budgeting properly and sticking to a budget for his leisure activities, and he never looked back.[38]

As soon as you learn and appreciate the benefits of guilt-free budgeting, you'll be able to live better and sleep better. Before you know it, the habit of guilt-free and intentional budgeting will already be ingrained in you, and when that time comes, *your financial security and success will be unstoppable!*

5 BUDGETING MISTAKES TO AVOID

- Starting late
- Failing to track monthly spending
- Not tying a financial goal into your budget
- Lack of budgeting method
- Not having fun money

KEY TAKEAWAYS

1. You have the right to spend guilt-free. The key is to make room for *'fun money'* in your monthly budget.

2. You may find budgeting restricting and laborious, but it's actually designed to help you understand and assess your relationship with money. It's a tool to help you reach your personal and financial goals.

3. Do remember that it takes trial and error to find the budgeting method that works for you. Aim to find and create a process that meets your needs, desires, and goals.

EXERCISE

Which budgeting method do you think will work for you? Choose one of the budgeting methods we discussed and create a budget using that method as a guide.

OPTION A: The 50-30-20 budgeting method

- 50% - Needs (Housing, utilities, groceries, health insurance, car payment)
- 30%- Wants (Shopping, hobbies, travel, entertainment, eating out)
- 20%- Savings (Savings, debt payments, investments)

OPTION B: The envelope method

Manage your finances by allocating specific amounts of cash into different envelopes.

OPTION C: Bullet journals

Create your budget journal or bullet journal. Start customizing how you'd want to track your income, expenses, savings, debt repayments, and financial goals. Write your reflections if you need to. Make it yours!

You can also choose some free budgeting apps to make the process even easier. Here are a few to check out:

- Mint (Best Free App for Personal Budgeting)
- Zeta (Best for Couples)
- GoodBudget (Best for Envelope System Budgeting)
- PocketGuard (Best for Overspenders)
- Empower (Best for Investment Tracking)

EXERCISE (continued)

There's no one-size fits all approach, and there are no rules in terms of budgeting methods. You can even create a hybrid method that is unique to your needs and preferences. Whatever that is, follow that process now and see how it works in your current situation. If it doesn't work, don't worry. You can always tweak and repeat as often as necessary.

Chapter 4

BE INSURED

This chapter is all about insurance, its importance, how it works, and the types of insurance plans you should be aware of. We'll also discuss how to choose the right insurance coverage that can help you and your family receive adequate coverage and financial support against life's vulnerabilities.

WHAT IS INSURANCE?

Insurance is a legal contract in which an individual or entity pays an insurance provider a premium in exchange for receiving reimbursement or financial protection against certain risks linked to one's life, health, or property. While the insurance policy may not always cover the full cost, it definitely will help make the payments more affordable. People usually secure insurance for their house, car, health, or life.

The concept of insurance actually dates back to the 18th century B.C. In ancient times, the first insurance policy was written on a Babylonian monument with the Code of Hammurabi.[4] The earliest accounts provided basic insurance, indicating that debtors didn't need to pay back loans in the event of personal disasters.

Since the beginning of time, the value of insurance has been central, helping individuals and businesses hedge against the risk of potential dangers and losses.

HOW INSURANCE WORKS

When you purchase an insurance policy, you'll have to make regular payments, also known as premiums, to the insurance company, usually on a monthly basis. If there's an unforeseen event covered by the policy, you can make a claim and the insurance company will cover the expenses or the loss as per the policy's terms and conditions.

If you don't make a claim, you will not be getting the premiums back. Instead, your regular payments will be pooled along with the payments of other policyholders from the same company. If you do make a claim, the money will be drawn from the huge pool of premiums from all policyholders.

INSURANCE POLICY COMPONENTS

You need to understand the components of an insurance policy, so you can carefully choose the right coverage for you, your family, or your property. Any insurance policy has three main components: **premium**, **policy limit**, and **deductible**. Let's go through each of them one by one.

Premium

The policy's premium is the price or monthly cost of the coverage. How insurers calculate the premium depends on the insurance type among other relevant factors. For example:

- **Car insurance** companies will look at your history of auto and property claims, creditworthiness, age, location, and other factors that may vary from state to state.
- **Health insurance** companies will check your health status, location, age, sex, tobacco and alcohol use, and coverage levels.
- **Home insurance** providers will look into your location, claims history, coverage amounts, personal belongings, and the value of your property.

- **Life insurance** providers will determine your age, health status, sex, tobacco and alcohol use, and amounts of coverage.

Insurance companies will generally assess your risk for a claim. For example, if you have a previous case of reckless driving, you will have to pay a higher monthly premium than someone with a perfect driving record. The insurance company will do some legwork to identify the right premium for your policy. The process involves actuarial science that uses statistical and mathematical models for quantifying risks and predicting outcomes. For example, by thoroughly analyzing past data, actuaries can determine that male drivers aged 15-24 are more likely to encounter serious accidents due to speeding.[5] With predictive information like this, insurance companies are better able to set premiums and policy limits to cover potential liabilities.

Policy limit

Every coverage has a policy limit. It's the maximum amount the insurance company will pay to cover the loss. It could be:

- Per loss or injury
- Per period (annual policy limit)
- Over the life of the policy (lifetime maximum)

The higher the limit, the more expensive the premium. If you reach the policy limit, you will have to personally cover the rest of the expenses. You are free to choose the policy limit, but in some cases, there are requirements set by the government or other parties. For instance, most states set a minimum amount of car insurance coverage. Thus, the policyholder's limit should be equal to or greater than the required limits. If you're free to choose the policy limit, consider the amount you would need in case the worst-case scenario happens. For example, if your home and all your belongings get destroyed by a fire incident, how much would you need to cover the entire damage? Depending on the policy limit you need, the insurance company will then calculate the premium and the deductible options.

Deductible

The deductible is the amount you'd have to pay out of pocket before the insurance company starts paying for the coverage. For instance, if you have health insurance coverage with a $1000 deductible and your medical bill is $2000, you need to pay the $1000 out of pocket before the insurer covers the rest.

Deductibles are usually reset for every policy period. For example, if you have a health insurance policy with an annual deductible of $1000, you need to pay that amount every year before the insurance company starts covering the health expenses *for that year*. This is a form of risk sharing between policyholders and insurers.

The higher the deductible, the lower the premium. The lower the deductible, the more expensive the price as well. Make sure to take into account your financial or personal situation when choosing a deductible. For instance, if you are still young and lead a healthy lifestyle, since you rarely need medical care, you may choose a higher deductible to save on the monthly costs. However, if you have a chronic medical condition and require frequent doctor visits, you may need a lower deductible to minimize out-of-pocket expenses. Also take into account your recreation and hobbies: Are you a rock climber? Do you enjoy skydiving on the weekends? Do you occasionally enter amateur skateboarding competitions? These high risk activities are a factor when considering insurance.

The deductibles vary depending on the type of coverage. Some companies even adopt a percentage-based deductible instead of a fixed one. Make sure to understand the scope and speak with a licensed insurance agent that can help you choose the right policy for your needs.

TYPES OF INSURANCE

In life, there are all sorts of unexpected situations. That is why there are many types of insurance to cover all kinds of setbacks and disasters. Let's discuss the most important ones that you should secure to have protection against life's unpleasant surprises.

Health Insurance

Health insurance offers coverage for medical costs related to an injury, illness, pregnancy, or even preventive care. The types of illnesses, treatments, and procedures covered will depend on the policy and the insurer's terms.

Studies show that about 4 in 10 Americans (41%) are burdened by debt due to medical or dental bills.[6] The rising healthcare costs also make some adults skip or delay seeking medical services. By getting health insurance, you get to share the financial burden with the insurance company to settle large medical bills.

Auto

Most states require auto insurance. There are different types of car insurance. Some will protect you, your passengers, and your vehicle while others can also cover injuries and damages of another party. The most common types of auto insurance include:

- **Collision Coverage**
  This covers the damages to your own vehicle if it gets involved in a car accident or collides with an object like a tree or a building even if you're at fault. However, it won't cover the damages to the other party's vehicle.

- **Comprehensive Coverage**
  This covers damages other than those incurred during a collision.

This includes fire damage, vandalism, hail damage, a cracked/ shattered windshield, damage from falling objects, etc. It will also reimburse you if your vehicle gets stolen.

- **Liability Car Insurance**
  This policy covers bodily injury or property damage in car accidents for which you are legally at fault. It only covers the damages to the other party and their property. Liability insurance is usually required in most states.

- **Uninsured/underinsured motorist**
  You would need this coverage if the other driver who is at fault doesn't have any liability coverage or doesn't have enough of it. This policy protects you from irresponsible motorists. It sucks when you'd have to pay out of pocket for an accident you didn't cause, so this type of insurance can come in handy.

- **Personal Injury Protection (PIP)**
  Personal Injury Protection is also called 'no-fault insurance'. In this coverage, it doesn't matter who is at fault. Your personal injuries and expenses in the event of a car accident will be covered, and it even extends to other drivers or household members you list on your policy. It's more comprehensive than MedPay and can even cover the loss of earnings due to an accident, childcare expenses, funeral costs, and more.

- **Medical Payments (MedPay)**
  MedPay is similar to PIP, but it has a narrower scope. It only covers the medical expenses for you, the passengers, and other policyholders. You can consider it a supplement to your health insurance.

Life Insurance

Life insurance is a contract and a guarantee that the insurance company will pay a lump sum, also called a death benefit, to the family or beneficiaries of the policyholder in the event of his/her death. The policyholder can pay a single life insurance premium upfront or pay premiums regularly over time.

There are two main categories of life insurance:

1. **Term Life Insurance.** Term life insurance only lasts for a specific term or period. It can be in force for 1, 5, 10 or even 30 years depending on the contract. The coverage will expire when that term ends. After which, you can choose to renew your policy. The payout will only be released if the policyholder dies during that specified period.

   When deciding the amount of coverage, make sure it covers the amount of debt such as the mortgage you'll be leaving behind so that your heirs will no longer have to worry about the payments.

2. **Permanent or Whole Life Insurance.** The other category is Permanent Life Insurance. It's also called whole life insurance or cash value life insurance. In this case, you are covered for your entire life as long as you keep paying your bill.

   Unlike term life insurance, wherein the policy will no longer have value once it expires, in whole life insurance, you can build cash value that can become a life-long asset. You can even take out loans against the cash value accumulated, but that will reduce the cash benefit.

   Permanent life insurance is more expensive than term insurance, but since it has a savings component with a fixed interest rate, it can be an attractive choice. Although the premium for permanent insurance can be more expensive, you can also go for this other type of permanent life insurance called Universal Life Insurance. This is a more flexible plan since you can increase or decrease the death benefit or adjust or even skip your monthly premium (within specific limits). The main difference between Whole and Universal life insurance is that the interest rate in universal coverage is not fixed. It may change depending on the market conditions.

Other types of permanent life insurance are Variable Life Insurance which is a bit riskier and Final Expense Insurance which basically covers end-of-life costs such as funeral expenses, hospital bills, and outstanding debt.

Life insurance is actually the cornerstone of proper financial planning. Especially if you have dependents, you can have peace of mind knowing that you and your loved ones are covered.

Renter's Insurance

Even if you don't have your own home, you can still secure coverage to protect your belongings. Your landlord's insurance policy may protect the building, but it doesn't cover your personal items. If you're renting an apartment, condo, or home, you can secure your belongings in case of theft, fire, and other insured disasters with your Renter's Insurance. Besides protecting your belongings from loss or damage, it can also cover you in case you're forced to temporarily move out of the property to cover the alternative living arrangements while waiting for the property to be repaired or rebuilt. Some renter's insurance also covers personal injury in case the insured disasters cause medical attention.

Renter's insurance does not cover expensive valuables, collectibles, motorized vehicles, and items from your home business such as a business laptop.

Home Insurance

Also called Homeowners Insurance, this coverage helps you secure your home, property structures, and personal belongings against unexpected damage, natural disasters, vandalism, or theft.

Besides mortgage companies requiring home insurance, it's highly recommended to have one because your home is your biggest personal investment, and you want it protected against any unforeseen events. There are four main things that a home insurance policy covers:

1. **Your property's physical structure.** In case your home is damaged or totally destroyed by fire, hail, hurricane, lightning, or other insured disasters, the policy covers the cost of repair. The ideal coverage should be enough to rebuild your home in case of major damages.

2. **The personal belongings inside your home.** This covers everything in your home be it furniture, clothes, sports equipment, and other personal items that are stolen or destroyed by insured disasters. Luxury items like jewelry, designer items, art, and collectibles can be covered, but there usually are dollar limits to these possessions. Motorized vehicles and business-related items are not usually covered as well.

3. **Liability protection.** This involves coverage in case of property damage or bodily injury lawsuits that you or your family members cause to other people. Even the damages caused by your pets can be covered.

4. **Coverage for Additional Living Expenses.** If your home becomes uninhabitable due to fire, storm, or other insured disasters, the ALE can cover the costs of your living expenses including temporary housing, travel costs, food expenses, utilities, and other basic living expenses.

    The benefits of having home insurance versus the risks of not having it are just too great to ignore. Secure your biggest asset and protect it with the right homeowner's insurance for your needs.

Travel Insurance

Travel insurance covers all financial losses related to travel including accidents, injury, theft or baggage loss, flight delays and cancellations, among other travel-related mishaps. The cost of travel insurance is usually 4-10% of the trip's price. Travel insurance, however, doesn't cover pre-existing health conditions, pregnancy and childbirth, or mishaps incurred from engaging in dangerous adventures/activities or those caused by political unrest. For a special vacation which often involves a group of people, one should purchase trip insurance with a CFAR rider (Cancel For Any Reason). This insurance allows you to recover 60-90% of the cost of the trip when canceled for literally any reason!

Choose the right insurance agent when purchasing any kind of insurance policy and never overlook the power of preparation. When researching insurance options and before sealing any deal, have the company explain in detail how to make a claim, Ask questions like "How long does it usually take to settle a claim?" or "What is the most common reason a claim is denied?" These, and other questions will help to avoid difficulties with your policy down the road.

A lot of financial burdens are a result of not being financially equipped. Insurance coverage serves as your buffer against life's unforeseen events, helping you become more in control and have better peace of mind.

THE EARLIER, THE BETTER

All the types of insurance discussed in the previous section are important and valuable. However, in this section, let's single out life insurance and why getting one as soon as possible is a wise financial move.

We talked about life insurance, particularly permanent life insurance, having an investment component. In the previous chapters, we highlighted the value of savings, investments, and financial freedom. The right life insurance coverage can become a crucial tool not only for safeguarding you (and a future family) but also for building wealth.

The following are some of the main benefits of getting life insurance as early as possible:

Get cheaper rates

Since a younger person has minimal risk of developing illnesses, younger policyholders get to pay lower premiums. Age is the primary factor when determining the price of a life insurance policy, so make sure to grab this chance to spend less and gain more.

Protect loved ones financially

Having life insurance is one of the best acts of love and care. In your 20's, people often start getting credit cards and taking loans to buy a car or townhouse/condominium. If anything bad happens to you, you'll be leaving behind financial burdens to your spouse, children, or aging parents. Even if you don't have a spouse or a kid yet, that could change in the future, and securing protection is something that you definitely won't regret.

Add more coverage later without the high cost

You may want to add extra benefits in the future when you start building your family or experience lifestyle changes. If you get life insurance earlier, you can customize your coverage and add rider features according to your needs *without the high cost.*

Receive money when you need it most

Many life insurance coverage also supports critical illness coverage. It's not just your beneficiaries that will receive the benefits. If you're caught up in an accident, surgery, or hospital confinement, some life insurance policies can also cover these hospital expenses. You would also receive your cash benefit in case of a major accident or total disability that disables you from working or supporting your family. This form of income replacement is critical for you and your family's future financial security.

Gain better investment returns and savings

If you buy a life insurance plan with investment and savings components, you will be building cash value that you can consider as your investment fund. You can also tap into that cash value in case of emergencies in the future

Take a proactive and responsible step towards future financial security and be insured to reap the best rewards later on.

TIPS FOR CHOOSING A LIFE INSURANCE POLICY

In order to secure adequate financial protection and coverage, you need to carefully choose the right life insurance policy that supports your needs and goals. The following are the steps to take in order to choose the best life insurance coverage:

Assess your life insurance goals.

If your primary goal is just to safeguard your family's financial security when you're gone, term insurance may be a good option as the premiums are more affordable and the coverage is pretty high.

Calculate the optimal insurance coverage that you need

Financial advisers would usually suggest aiming for life insurance coverage that's 10-15 times your yearly income. However, remember that there are other factors to consider. If you have debts or if your children are still schooling, it might be more challenging for your family to handle the burdens when you're gone, especially if you're the main breadwinner.

To get the optimal insurance coverage, calculate the following:

- Your family's yearly expenses multiplied by the number of years for which income replacement is necessary
- The total amount of debts you have including mortgages
- The amount you want to secure for your child's future education expenses or even wedding costs among other future considerations

Determine the amount you need to pay as a premium and look for the policy that offers the best deal

There are a lot of premium calculators you can use online to get an estimate on how much you'd have to pay monthly for your ideal life insurance coverage. Compare all the plans available and look for the policy that offers the best coverage at rates that suit your budget. Don't forget to think about possible events that could happen like sudden unemployment. Consider your earnings for the incoming years and set-tle for a policy that meets your goals and, at the same time, is feasible budget-wise.

Select the correct policy term

When deciding the policy term or period, consider the number of years your family will have to be financially dependent on you. There's this general rule of thumb that involves subtracting your current age from the tentative age you'd stop generating income.

Opt for a reputable life insurance provider

To make sure that your investment is in good hands, check the insurance company's financial solvency. There are insurance rating agencies like Fitch Ratings, A.M. Best, Moody's and S&P that you can check to gauge the company's ability to settle future claims. Check online reviews and feedback on independent websites and forums. You can also check your state insurance department to verify the insurance company's licensing as well as any regulatory actions and complaints filed against them.

Do not conceal facts from your life insurance provider

If you have pre-existing illnesses or a family history of critical illnesses, be transparent and don't conceal these details. The same thing if you consume alcohol or tobacco or work in a high-risk job. Concealing the facts is just bound to cause claim rejection when the time comes.

Read the final policy document carefully

Read the full contract including the fine print. Check the important details like the lock-in period and the circumstances that make a claim invalid. The lock-in period is the time frame (i.e 5 years) when the policy-holder won't be able to liquidate or withdraw the total funds accumulated.

Just don't rush the process and take your time finding the best coverage for you and your family.

Buy life insurance at an early age

As mentioned in the previous section, there are a lot of advantages to buying life insurance earlier than later. As soon as you start earning, consider purchasing life insurance to pay lower premiums and add riders more affordably in the future.

Choose a comprehensive plan

Enhance your coverage by adding rider options to your policy. The following are some common riders you can explore to achieve a more comprehensive plan:

- Critical Illness
- Child Term
- Permanent Disability
- Accidental Death Benefit
- Terminal Illness

Choose rider functions that match your needs and lifestyle and up-grade your life insurance coverage and financial protection for you and your beneficiaries. Don't forget about the life insurance offered by your employer. Often, it'll be cheap or your employer actually pays the premiums for the lowest coverage!

Evaluate your life insurance needs regularly
Your priorities and financial goals may change over time. When you get married or have kids, you need to make the necessary adjustments that match your new life and your new goals.

THE REAL WORLD . . . Take for example the story of an 18-year old, who went to Hawaii to spend time with family and learn how to surf for the first time in November of 2021. During a surf lesson, his lower back felt tense and his legs suddenly gave out. There was no trauma or accident, whatsoever. He felt the symptoms of a rare condition called Surfer's Myelopathy. It was so rare that only 100 cases have been documented in the past 20 years.[25] He ended up being paralyzed and had to go through extensive spinal rehabilitation. The condition is also rarely covered by the insurance, but luckily, his father had purchased an accident rider the previous year and that covered this young man's case. *His father assessed the risk associated with his son's lifestyle and activities, including amateur skateboarding, and he anticipated that additional coverage was necessary.* Smart investing at work!

Insurance plays a critical role in financial planning, and before you think about investments, it's best to first secure the right insurance policies to avoid draining your savings account when financial setbacks arise. *Be insured and establish your safety net today!*

5 INSURANCE MISTAKES TO AVOID

- Starting late
- Not having insurance goals
- Failing to assess and calculate the right insurance coverage
- Working with the wrong insurance provider
- Not evaluating your insurance needs regularly

KEY TAKEAWAYS

1. Being insured is your best bet for overcoming life's uncertainties.

2. You need to understand the components of an insurance policy, so you can carefully choose the right coverage for you, your family, or your property.

3. Explore all the types of insurance available and maximize the ones that can better protect you from possible setbacks or disasters.

EXERCISE

If you don't have life insurance yet, it's about time to get covered. Before anything else, make sure you complete the steps below:

1. **Check your employers life insurance offerings.** If you did not opt in at the time of employment, find out when the next enrollment opportunity is and be sure to take advantage of it if it fits into your needs, usually this is the cheapest and best life insurance available to you.

2. **Calculate the optimal insurance coverage:** multiply your yearly income by 10. If you have other financial burdens underway, multiply it higher like 15-20 times. For a more accurate gauge, you can also add up the following:

   • Your family's annual expenses multiplied by the number of years for which income replacement is necessary

   • The total amount of debts you have

   • The total amount you want to secure for your children's education or other future expenses.

3. **Check the premium you would need to pay for** to achieve the ideal coverage, and assess whether or not it's something you can afford. Make sure to compare all plans available to get the best deal. As much as possible, add relevant riders to achieve a comprehensive plan. These include:

   • Critical Illness
   • Child Term
   • Permanent Disability
   • Accidental Death Benefit
   • Terminal Illness

4. **Choose the right insurance company with an established reputation and review your coverage regularly** as your life conditions change. Look up several insurance companies to see their ratings within the industry: Fitch Ratings, A.M. Best, Moody's and S&P's. Also check your state insurance department to verify different company's licensing as well as any regulatory actions and complaints filed against them.

Chapter 5

DEALING WITH DEBT

$\mathcal{N}$ot all debts are bad. For instance, a mortgage is crucial to achieving your goal of becoming a homeowner. Properties also appreciate in value, which can be a form of investment. However, there are also the wrong kinds of debt such as high-interest credit card debt.

If you're struggling to pay off debt and you're adding more debt to the pile, you should not ignore the situation but rather, deal with it before it gets out of hand. Debt elimination actually comes before investments in the **financial freedom pyramid**. It's a core foundation of financial wellness. In this chapter, we're going to explore all the ways you can manage debt **and lead a** debt-free life.

EFFECTS OF DEBT

Carrying debt is not the problem. It's all about the kind of debt you're accumulating and how you handle debt in general. If you're still paying for the debt you accumulated last month, last year,

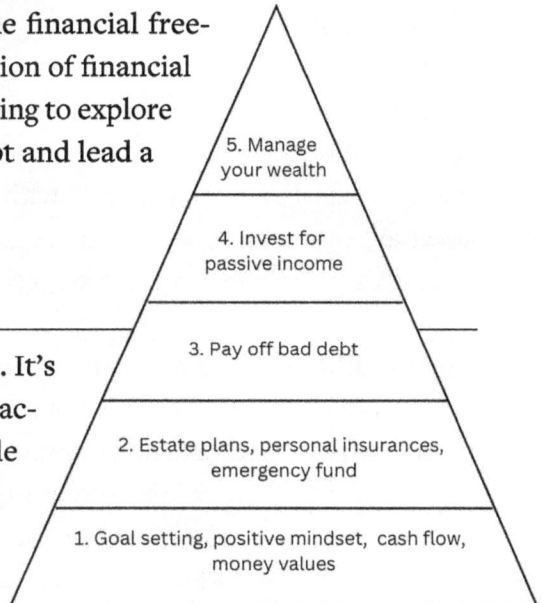

5. Manage your wealth

4. Invest for passive income

3. Pay off bad debt

2. Estate plans, personal insurances, emergency fund

1. Goal setting, positive mindset, cash flow, money values

or even a decade ago, that long-term debt can have negative consequences on your finances.

The following are the specific consequences you might face if your debt is not managed properly.

Paying more than an item costs

If you bought a $2000 Miele dishwasher on credit at an 11% interest rate and chose to pay $50 over 48 months, the total cost of the appliance + interest is worth $2400 by the time it's paid off. Imagine the opportunity cost of the $400 interest. While it makes sense to use credit for items you can't afford yet, *if you're overly dependent on credit cards,* that could turn into an unhealthy habit that could harm your finances. In a situation like this, if you have a good credit score, you can probably find a store that will give you X number of months interest free. Thus you sign up for their credit card and immediately after the purchase set up an automatic monthly payment to pay the balance off before the interest kicks in!

Lower credit score

One of the main factors that determine your credit score is the amount of debt you're carrying. Your level of debt constitutes 30% of your credit score. The bigger the credit balance in relation to the credit limit, the lower the credit score. Accounts with over-the-limit or maxed-out balances are the worst case. If your credit score is low, you'll have a harder time taking out loans to purchase a car or a house.

The inability to own a home

When shopping for a condo, a house, or other real estate and applying for a loan, the lenders will examine all of your existing debts— from auto loans to credit cards to student loans. A report published by the National Association of Realtors shows that 50% of the people who have not purchased a home yet, consider their student debt as the main culprit for the delay.[7] If that's the case, you would have to rent for longer which can be more expensive than paying for a monthly mortgage. Years ago, our nanny shared with us what she and her husband paid for rent. We were surprised that it was higher than our mortgage. We introduced them to our mortgage banker and within 4 months they purchased their first home and their mortgage was smaller than their previous rent! They were able to do this because they had little debt and a good credit score.

Stress and serious medical problems

Debt doesn't only affect your financial well-being. It also impacts your mental, physical, and emotional health.[8] According to Bankrate, among the respondents who claimed that money is affecting their mental health, 47 percent say that managing debt is their primary issue.[9] Moreover, according to AIMS Public Health, people carrying debt are also three times more likely to experience stress, anxiety, and depression.[10]

Debt stress has been shown to cause various health issues like muscle tension, migraines, high blood pressure, stomach ulcers, insomnia, and heart attacks.[11] Debt and financial hardships are also risk factors for suicide.[12] They're also a common cause of money disagreements and conflicts among many marriages and families.

To lead a more stress-free life, debt management is key. Deal with the money problems head-on, make a plan to pay off debt, and make the necessary lifestyle and habit changes that can help restore your financial health.

Unable to retire

If you're still carrying consumer debt into retirement, that could harm your monthly cash flow upon retirement, and your healthcare, leisure, and travel budgets will be affected. Your retirement accounts may drain faster than planned and you may run out of money or need to adjust your lifestyle just to make ends meet. The goal is to ensure that your retirement fund outlives you and you can continue living a comfortable lifestyle after your working years.

That is why as early as now, stay away from bad debt. Control your spending habits today and as much as possible, *use debt to fuel your financial standing.* Instead of accumulating debt for your handbag collection, perhaps it's best to use debt to support actual assets and investments or cover business expenses. *In short, do your best to only use debt to pay for things that can help you grow.* Don't use it to buy random things you can't afford.

ESTABLISHING CREDIT

Establishing credit while you're young can ease your transition to adulthood. It can help you with your first milestones as a full-fledged adult— like your first car or mortgage loan, your first apartment, or even your first job. Your credit score predominantly determines your future. Just remember, low credit scores mean higher interest rates, and conversely, high credit scores mean lower interest rates.

The longer you have credit, the higher the chances of building a good credit score. An excellent credit score can help you with the following:

Leasing an apartment
Landlords may check your credit score to make sure that you are a responsible tenant and pay bills on time. Not having a credit report to show may lead to application rejection or may require a creditworthy cosigner or a hefty security deposit.

Setting up utilities
Even utility companies ask for applicants' Social Security numbers and verify tenants' credit reports. A poor credit score may make it hard to obtain these services or may necessitate paying a deposit. That being said, you should generally avoid giving out your Social Security number

to any organization other than banking or investment institutions. Usually, other businesses (utilities, medical offices) have another way to create an ID for you.

Applying for a job

Employers may also look into candidates' credit history to ensure that they're responsible and trustworthy people. In fact, 29% of employers do these credit checks when filling certain positions, especially those involving bookkeeping, accounts management, and bank transactions.[13]

Buying a car

Around 81% of Americans have car loans, and if you intend to go this route along with the majority of car owners, you need to establish your credit history.[14] If not, you will need a creditworthy cosigner or you'll be paying higher interest on the loan. Or worse, your loan application will be denied. If you establish credit earlier, you can make the process easier and receive better interest rates as well.

Buying a house

If you're still in your early 20's, buying a house, townhouse, or condominium may be a far-fetched idea. However, securing a good credit score as early as today can help you easily qualify for a mortgage when the time comes. You can also secure lower interest rates if you have a good credit score. *That could save you tens of thousands of dollars over the span of a 30-year mortgage.*

Getting a cell phone

When signing up for your own account or financing your devices, many cell phone providers actually do a credit check. Your financial stability and credit history will be examined before getting the 12 months or 24 months contract.

Receiving better interest rates on credit cards and loans

Whether you're applying for a credit card or any loans, the lenders will look into your credit report to check your eligibility and determine the appropriate interest rate. The higher the credit score, the more likely the approval and, as usual, better the interest rates.

HOW TO BUILD CREDIT IN YOUR 20'S

Your 20's are actually the perfect time to supercharge your financial journey by taking care of some legwork including building credit.

Where and how do you begin? Let's explore all the ways you can build and keep a good credit score in your 20's.

Check your credit score

Even if you've never had credit before, it's still important to request your credit report from each of the major credit bureaus including Experian, Equifax, and TransUnion. There are cases of identity theft and you need to make sure that there are no opened accounts using your name. According to a report from the 2021 Child Identity Fraud Study by Javelin Strategy & Research, over 1.25 million children suffered from identity fraud in 2020.[15] You need to verify that you're starting with a clean slate, and the earlier you can detect discrepancies, the earlier you can report it and take action. For a free credit report, start with your local bank, wherever you have your checking or savings account.

Open a student credit card

There are a lot of credit cards on the market, and some banks also offer student credit cards. Their credit limit is lower, and the APR rate is higher than the usual credit card, but this option doesn't require an established credit history. Many of these types of cards also offer student-related perks. Just use it for the main purpose of starting your credit history as early as possible and establishing your score beforehand by paying on time, keeping credit usage low, and using your credit card responsibly.

Apply for a secured credit card

A secured credit card requires a cash deposit, which serves as the account's collateral, offering the issuer security in case the cardholder cannot make payments. The cash deposit becomes the credit limit, and it's refundable as long as you repay your credit card balance. As you use the credit card, your payments will be reported to the credit bureaus, helping you establish a good credit record early on. The point is to build a good credit history, so make sure to play your cards right and don't miss any payments.

Make your payments online

In a NerdWallet survey, the report shows that 33% of Americans said that they missed their credit card payments because they didn't have the money, but 35% said that they missed just because they forgot.[16] Taking care of your credit score is one of the best financial moves you can make. Don't let bad memory get in the way by considering automatic payments online through your bank account. The smartest option here is to log into your credit card and set up *minimum autopay*, thus building good credit and never missing a payment (you should always make additional payments every month and move towards 100% payoff each month).

Keep your credit usage low

As much as 30% of your credit score depends on your **credit utilization ratio.** It's a measure of how much of your credit limit you're using. As a rule of thumb, the lower your credit usage, the better. To calculate your credit ratio, just divide your total credit card balances by your total credit limits. Your credit card utilization ratio should be under 30%. Low credit card usage is a sign that you're not relying on credit cards too much and you're handling it responsibly.

Securing your financial future involves a lot of things. Building and managing credit is definitely one of the key foundations. Young people can reap maximum advantages if they start preparing as early as possible. The earlier you get on top of things, the better.

MISTAKES TO AVOID

Credit cards can be such a great alternative to cash, and they can come to your rescue when you find yourself in a pinch. As long as you pay your balances off every month, you don't need to pay any interest, and when you use it right, it can build your credit score which can benefit a lot of areas of your life.

Unfortunately, Americans have racked up so much credit card debt. According to the Federal Reserve Bank, credit card debt in the US hit an all-time high of $986 billion in 2023.[17] This is mainly because of credit card misuse among cardholders, which can be alleviated by taking proactive steps and acquiring more financial knowledge and responsibility.

The following are some of the common mistakes people make in terms of credit card usage:

Going overboard

Just because you qualify for multiple credit cards, it doesn't mean you need to keep too many of them. That will just complicate your finances, and whenever you apply for a new credit card, the issuer will conduct a hard inquiry to obtain your entire credit history. According to FICO, a hard inquiry can typically lower a credit score by less than 5 points, but there are cases when the decrease is as much as 10 points.[18] Plus, lenders may view you as a high-risk customer if you have too many hard inquiries in a short period. The maximum number of credit cards you should have is three.

Maxing out your credit

Maxing out your credit card can pose a lot of issues for you. Your credit score will decrease, your minimum payments will increase, and you'll pay for additional fees and penalties. In the next section, we'll talk more about how to avoid such a scenario and how to manage your finances better.

Missing a payment

When you miss or delay your credit card payment, you'll incur a late payment fee, a possible interest spike, and a credit score hit especially if it's over 30 days late. As soon as you realize you missed a payment, pay the minimum amount as soon as possible, or contact your issuer to request a modified due date or a reduced interest rate or payment plan. There's no guarantee, but it won't hurt to ask. Any reported missed or late payments leave a black mark on your credit history that could affect you for years, so basically, sign up for auto-pay and avoid this situation entirely!

Closing accounts prematurely

Another credit card mistake is closing accounts prematurely. Even if you're no longer using a credit card, you may still want to keep it open. First of all, closing it won't stop the interest from accruing or won't make the balance go away. The issuer will still expect it to be paid. And even if you have already repaid the outstanding balance, it's still recommended to keep the account open to boost your credit utilization ratio over the months or years of not using the card. You can also just take it out of your wallet and store in a secure place. That way it is working for you to boost your utilization ratio and credit score as well as not increasing debt. That's a smart money move!

MANAGING STUDENT LOANS

Graduating college is supposed to be fun, but it's rather hard to celebrate when hefty student loans are attached to your diploma. However, don't lose hope because there are a lot of actionable strategies for paying off your student loans sooner than you think.

Let's navigate the crucial steps for effectively paying off your student loan debt.

Calculate your total debt

When managing any kind of debt, the first step is to always know how much you owe. This way, you can develop a strategy to pay your debt down, consolidate it, or even apply for debt forgiveness which we will further discuss in the next pages.

Know the terms

You can make more informed decisions and navigate your financial journey better if you learn the ins and outs of student loans and get familiar with the terms. In the next few pages, we shall highlight some of the important terms to know and understand, including graduated repayment, extended repayment, PAYE, loan forgiveness, and so on.

Review the grace periods

After graduation, you're not expected to start paying your student loans right away. For federal loans, the grace period is usually 6 months, but for private student loans, the exact duration can vary. You don't want accidental missed payments after the grace period, so you need to keep the grace period in mind and prepare accordingly.

Consider consolidation

Students who take out loans typically borrow from 8-10 different lenders by the time they graduate. Student loan consolidation involves combining several student loans into one big loan from a single lender. The bigger loan will be used to pay off all the other loans. Interest rates will play a large factor here. If your multiple student loan rates are significantly lower than a consolidation loan rate, it is better to keep the lower interest loans *and set up automatic payments* (and *always* pay a bit more than minimum (even $5-$20 more each month will reduce the overall length of the loan)).

If the interest rates make sense,this process can help simplify and reduce your monthly payments as it offers alternative payment plans to make the overall debt more manageable. According to CNBC Select, borrowers save $4000 to $7000 over the life of their loan if they sign up for private student loan consolidation.[19]

There are two main ways to consolidate your education loans.

- *Federal student loan consolidation:* You can apply for Direct Consolidation Loan under the US. Department of Education. This only applies to federal loans— private loans can't be included.
- *Private student loan consolidation:* You can combine all student loans, private or federal, by refinancing your education loans with a credit union or private lender.

Hit higher-interest loans first

This approach applies to all kinds of debt. This is also called the **"avalanche method"** for debt management. The higher-interest loans will cost more over time, and paying off these loans first can help you save a lot in the long run. Just make minimum payments on all other outstanding accounts, but use the rest of your extra money to pay off the one with the highest interest.

Pay down principal

Don't just make the minimum payments month by month. Make sure to make extra payments towards the principal balance. You can save a lot on interest if you manage to pay down the principal. For example, if your student loan debt is $35,000 with a 6.8% interest rate and $403 minimum payment. If you only make the minimum payments, you'll pay off your student loan in 10 years with a whopping $13,324 in total interest. If you manage to increase your payment to $500 a month, you can save $3,613 in interest over the life of your loan, as well as reducing the loan length (you may be able to shave off a full year of payments). *That's a big difference!*

Check your account statements and verify if the lender has correctly applied the extra payment to the principal amount. If not, contact the lender and make sure that your future payments are applied accurately. With many institutions moving towards paperless statements, be sure you are checking all your statements once per month to verify correct application of payments and review your progress.

Pay automatically

Some federal and private student loans *provide a discount* on the interest rate if you set up the monthly payments automatically from your checking account. For example, the Federal Direct Loan Program offers a 0.25% discount on interest, which can already mean huge savings over time. This is a no-brainer– ALWAYS take advantage of this offering!

Explore alternative plans

For those taking out federal student loans, there are alternative repayment plans you can explore. The following are the common ones:

- **Graduated repayment**
  This plan starts with lower payments which would gradually increase every two years. This is perfect for fresh graduates with entry-level salaries. The loan should be repaid in 10 to 30 years. Since the payments will increase over time, the ideal scenario is you eventually get a pay raise or move on to a better-paying job.

- **Extended repayment**

  This lowers your monthly payments as you stretch out the loan over a longer term, such as 25 years instead of 10 years. Extending the life of your loan means paying more interest, but if your goal is to make your monthly payments more manageable, this alternative plan can be a great choice. Once you feel like you can afford higher monthly payments, you can also adjust your repayment plan accordingly.

- **Income contingent repayment**

  Income Contingent Repayment (ICR) is an income-driven repayment plan. Your monthly payment depends on your AGI or Adjusted Gross Income. The payment amount should not be higher than 20% of your income for 25 years. At the end of the 25-year period, any debt balance will be forgiven. Since the repayment length is longer, the loan accrues more interest, but the loan forgiveness guarantee and the more affordable payments make it a sensible choice for some.

- **Pay as you earn**

  This is another income-driven repayment plan, capping your student loan at only 10% of your discretionary income. The repayment length is 20 years, and after that term, the rest of the loan balance will be forgiven. This plan is only for those who borrowed their first federal student loan after October 1, 2007. If you don't qualify for PAYE, there's another similar option called REPAYE. It's still at a 10% payment cap, but your balances will be forgiven after 25 years instead of 20— unless the loan was purely for undergraduate study.

- **Defer payments**

  Deferring payments allows you to temporarily suspend your monthly payments for up to three years. For subsidized federal loans, no interest will accrue over the deferment period, but for unsubsidized loans, expect that the interest will accrue. Deferment is the right choice if you are in a temporary financial bind and need more breathing room. However, if your loan is unsubsidized and the interest is expected to accrue, perhaps you can first explore income-driven repayment plans like PAYE or ICR.

- **Explore loan forgiveness**
  If your loans are forgiven, you won't have to pay back some or all of your balances. The most common way to apply for loan forgiveness is via Public Service Loan Forgiveness. There are a lot of ways to qualify for loan forgiveness.
  You can qualify if you are a:
  - Nonprofit worker
  - Teacher
  - Government employee
  - Nurse, doctor, or medical professional
  - Person with disability
  - Federal Perkins loan borrower
  - Parent borrower
  - Victim of forgery
  - You can also qualify if:
  - You repay your student loans under any income-driven repayment plan.
  - Your school has closed or misled you.
  - You've declared bankruptcy.
  - You're discharged due to death.

It's better to explore these alternative payment plans than to default on your loan or miss any payments. Explore your options to manage your finances better and successfully make your way towards becoming debt-free!

AVOID GETTING INTO DEBT

To actually make financial progress, it's important to avoid getting into debt as much as possible, especially consumer debt and payday loans. Let's explore all the ways you can avoid getting into debt and set yourself up for financial freedom.

If you can't afford it, don't buy it.
Your credit limit is not your money. Buying things you don't need using the money you don't have is a recipe for financial disaster. If you can't pay for it with cash, don't buy it! Sorry, but somebody had to say it!!??

Have an emergency fund.
Without an emergency fund, you'll have to resort to debt. Your emergency fund should be 6 months' worth of salary saved up. This can help you avoid financial distress should you lose your job, get sick, or experience anything unexpected that could affect your finances.

Pay off your credit card balances in full.
In Chapter 2, we talked about the importance of paying credit cards in full every month, and that piece of advice should be emphasized. Ditch the interest charges, protect your credit score, and avoid the cycle of debt that will only harm your financial future.

Cut out the wants and focus on the needs.
Needs are apparently the things you need to survive; wants are those you can comfortably live without. This does not mean you should never spend on wants. It's all about proper budgeting. In Chapter 3, we talked about securing 'fun money'. Just make sure to stick to the fun money budget and avoid splurging on sheer fun with your credit card.

Everything's better with a budget.
We wrote a whole chapter on budgeting because it's the simplest practice that can maintain order in your finances. Without a budget, it's easy to amass debt and spend more than you can afford. Without a budget, you can't secure the money you need for savings and investments. If you want financial freedom, budgeting is your best friend!

Do not use your credit card for cash advances.
Don't use your credit card to withdraw cash from an ATM. Cash advances via credit card are a very expensive type of transaction. You'll have to pay a cash advance fee which is either a fixed rate or a percentage of the cash advance. For example, it could be a flat fee of $5 or 5% of the amount. Not to mention the interest rates for cash advances are generally higher than regular transactions. That being said, sometimes credit cards will offer 0% balance transfers. This means they want you to pay off other credit cards with a check issued by them. And they give you 0% interest on the money for X number of months. Again, this can be a great way to consolidate, save interest and pay off debt quickly. However, you must understand the terms, and again, set up automatic payments to insure you pay it off in the time frame of the offer. Also be sure to understand how your current balance on the card is affected by the transfer.

Limit the number of cards you have.
If you have too many open credit lines, you'll appear like a high-risk borrower in the eyes of lenders. It's also even harder to control your spending and keep track of monthly payments and due dates when you have too many credit cards under your name. Though, if you don't intend to abuse these credit cards, that could benefit your credit utilization ratio and earn you more credit card rewards. Just weigh the pros and cons and think about whether or not you can handle the avoidable complication.

Secure a master sheet of expenses.

Whether you're using a spreadsheet, an app, or other money management tools, it's important to have a master sheet of your expenses that you update periodically (every month if possible). Track the balances and due dates and don't miss any payments. Update the sheet if you have any new monthly expenses, and while you're at it, make a general evaluation of your current financial situation. As you implement the theories in this book, you will also see progress each month! This movement towards financial freedom will bring great satisfaction, peace of mind, and allow you to begin *enjoying* true financial freedom.

Avoid lifestyle inflation

When you get a pay raise, instead of bloating your expenses to match your increased spending power, live off the lower salary and invest the new income: pay off debt, contribute to that emergency fund, or make a larger contribution to that vacation fund! Be smarter about your finances, so you can make the most of your hard-earned income.

Collect coupons to save cash.

Especially for items that you already planned to purchase, using coupons can reduce everyday expenses by 5-25%. Any freed-up cash can already go a long way if you have a huge debt to pay or a financial goal you badly want to achieve.

CONCLUSION

Dealing with finances can be overwhelming, but as long as you adopt healthy financial habits and avoid the common pitfalls that could harm your finances, you're on the right track. Prepare early, be wise about your spending and money matters, and guard your credit score like a hawk. As young adults, there are a lot of things you can do to keep your finances in check. It takes some determination and sacrifice, but it's all going to be worth it.

THE REAL WORLD . . . Take, for example, the story of Zina Kumok, a 26-year old marketing specialist from Indianapolis. She's only making $30,000 a year but managed to pay down $28,000 of her student loans in just three years. She was so committed to dealing with her debt now rather than later that she set aside 50% of her take home pay towards her student debt. For her, nothing is more liberating than paying her loans quickly, even if that means watching her friends go out and spend all they want. Until now, her *new* ability to delay gratification has brought her the financial rewards she well deserves.[37] Be inspired, you can do it too!

Adulting can be hard, but it doesn't have to be if you are well-equipped and well-disciplined. Don't get caught in the cycle of debt that over 340 million Americans live in.[20] Choose financial freedom and peace of mind by putting your finances in order as early as today!

5 CREDIT MISTAKES TO AVOID

- Having to many credit cards (2 is ideal, 3 is maximum)
- Maxing out your credit cards
- Missing monthly payments
- Closing credit card accounts prematurely
- Not establishing credit

KEY TAKEAWAYS

1. Paying off bad debt should be one of your main priorities if you want to improve your financial situation.

2. Having too much debt can have serious repercussions like the inability to buy a house, poor credit score, and even stress and health issues.

3. To prepare for the future, it's best to start building your credit while you're still young. Students can open a student or secured credit card and start using it to establish their credit score by making payments on time and keeping the credit utilization ratio low.

Let's start your journey to becoming debt-free! Follow the steps below and let's start eliminating debt, one loan at a time:

1. Identify your highest-interest loan.

2. Make the minimum payments for the rest of your loans, but save an additional $200 per month to pay down the principal of that high-interest loan.

3. Set up automatic payments for *all* debts.

4. Try this out for at least one year to establish new financial habits that can help you regain control of your finances!

Chapter 6

MULTIPLE STREAMS OF INCOME

*L*et's face it, it's downright risky to rely on a single source of income. Unexpected things are bound to happen— company layoffs, economic downturns, and other unforeseen life events. That's why having multiple streams of income is the ideal scenario. If you're diversifying your income stream, you're spreading out the risk and you have more resources to fall back on. If you do it right, some of the other streams of income could even turn out to be your main source of income. It's about applying the right strategy and *slowly but surely* building your wealth and financial freedom.

A LONG-TERM STRATEGY FOR WEALTH

Most people only have one primary source of income. That's not bad, but if financial health and freedom are what you're after, having multiple streams of income is the right strategy.

According to the IRS, the average millionaire has at least 7 streams of income.[21] Let's discuss each of those streams of income and how you can build them for yourself.

7 Common Income Streams of Millionaires

1. Dividend income

If you buy company stocks and become a shareholder, you can earn dividend income or a portion of the company's profits, usually paid every quarter or every year. Dividend investing is a low-risk approach and a long-term strategy for wealth building.

In the stock market, not all companies pay a dividend, so if you are interested in dividend investing, make sure to do your research and buy shares from companies with dividend payouts. This way, you won't rely on capital gains, and you can build wealth more easily by *reinvesting your dividend income* and letting compounding magic do the work (when you buy a stock like this there is an automatic way to reinvest the dividend, which automates the entire investment!).

2. Rental income

Rental income is a passive source of income because you don't need to do a lot besides collecting rent checks! You still need to do some work like finding tenants and managing the property, but once that's sorted out, money will just roll in month after month. Rental income is a great option for wealth building because it offers a solid and steady cash flow. Not to mention that property values generally increase over time, which means huge profit if you decide to sell it in the future. If you do not want to actively manage the property (or multiple properties), you can always employ a property management company (they will usually take a percentage of rent collected).

If you don't like managing properties, you can also just invest in REIT or Real Estate Investment Trust. REITs are publicly traded companies that finance, own, and operate income-generating real estate such as office buildings, apartments, and even shopping malls. This way, you can make the most of the real estate market without being a landlord!

3. Earned income

Earned income is the least passive way to make money. It's the income you get from employment or being self-employed by offering freelance services. With this type of income, to earn more, you'd have to work more. However, earned income is a core part of your financial goals. *Ideally, you should use your earned income to build assets that generate passive income.* It could be buying rental properties, investing in dividend stock, or building a more profitable business.

To get there faster, try to increase your earned income by getting the highest-paying job you can or perhaps asking for a raise. You can also choose to work freelance and charge more for your services while having more flexibility for building secondary income streams.

If you have a spouse, his/her salary is part of your family's earned income. It would be better if you work in different industries for better income diversity. For example, if you and your spouse work in the same company or industry, should something go wrong in the sector, your primary source of income could be in jeopardy. When spouses both work, ideally the family unit should live off of only 1 income, allowing the other income to pay off bad debt, invest, or create other income streams.

4. Royalties

This is the type of income you get from your patents, copyrights, trademarks, and other intellectual properties. For instance, if you invent a unique and useful type of widget and sell the patent to a company, you will be paid royalties each time they use your creation. If you write books, you will also receive royalties from the publisher for every book sold. You only need to put in the work upfront, and your creation can bring you passive income for the long term. The goal is to create something of value, something that people want and need.

5. Business income

Business income is the revenue you generate from operating a business. There are lots of types of businesses you can run. The following are some of the lucrative business ideas:

- **A service-based business**
  Your service-based business can offer expertise, skills, or labor to meet customer demands. That could be graphic design or copywriting, or it could be landscaping or home cleaning. It's now easier than ever to start and scale service-based businesses. You can build a website or app and launch targeted marketing campaigns online to supercharge your business and earn more profits! You can even simply join existing marketplaces to gain instant exposure. Be a market watcher and see where an entry may be timely: In the spring of 2020, at the start of the COVID pandemic, a young dad started a cleaning service that catered to businesses and worked at night. In less than 60 days he had lucrative contracts with Target, Hyvee, and others. In the spring of 2022 he sold the business for $1.2 million..... Not bad for a 2 year investment!

- **A product-based business**
  You can sell any kind of products online or in a physical store or even in a mobile truck. You can sell clothing, furniture, electronics, food items or any other physical product and take care of supply, inventory, marketing, and quality control to get the business going and hopefully turn it into a lucrative income source.

- **A franchise**
  There's a franchising opportunity in almost every industry. The key is to narrow down your options and choose the best one that suits your budget, interest, and skill set. You need to weigh your options well because most franchise agreements are multiyear contracts,

from 5 to 25 years. Make sure that you're up for a long-term commitment and choose something that will still interest you in the future. Some of the most profitable franchises in the US include Dunkin Donuts, McDonald's, 7-Eleven, Subway and so on.

- **Online business**
  There are so many ways to build a business online such as dropshipping, blogging, affiliate marketing, content creation, online consulting, course creation, and so on. Creating a strong online presence is key, and although that may take time and effort, it can become a sustainable source of revenue with the potential of tapping a global audience and various markets. If you can't commit full-time to building a business, you can start with a hobby business or a side business. It's best to choose a pursuit that you genuinely enjoy to make the process fun and rewarding for you.

6. Interest income

Interest income is the money earned from lending your funds to someone else or putting your money into a bank's deposit account. You can also invest in bonds and receive interest income from the bond issuer. Bonds mature at different time horizons, anywhere from 6 months to 10 years, lots of options here! This is another great way to generate passive income without lifting a finger! Just make sure that you're investing in reliable and safe investment options that release consistent interest payments.

7. Capital gains

Capital gains refer to the profits you make from selling a capital asset like real estate, stocks, precious metals, and other investments. For example, if you buy stock from Tesla for $150 and sell it for $200, your capital gain is $50. This is another passive income source but requires patience and the ability to play the game long-term.

REASONS TO HAVE MULTIPLE INCOME STREAMS

In this uncertain world, building multiple income streams is no longer a matter of luxury. It's now a necessity to create a more secure financial position. If you're still starting out, you don't have to pursue and get overwhelmed by the 7 income sources we talked about. Your job right now is to understand the need for creating a new income source and focus on adding at least one additional source of income in the next 2 years.

The following are the big reasons for creating multiple income sources for yourself and for your family:

Rising healthcare costs

The United States has the most expensive healthcare in the world.[22] The total healthcare spending in the country reached over $4.3 trillion in 2021, which is around $12,900 per person. The average healthcare cost in other developed countries is only half as much. Despite the higher healthcare spending, the health outcomes are not any better than those in other wealthy countries. If anything, the US is performing worse in terms of infant mortality, life expectancy, and unmanaged diabetes.[23]

With the country's dysfunctional healthcare system, an additional income source can go a long way to cover unexpected medical expenses and prepare for life's surprises.

Possible layoffs

No job is perfectly safe or stable. In the past few years, even the big tech powerhouses laid off hundreds and thousands of employees. In the first 5 months of 2023, there were a total of 15.4 million layoffs in the US, and 48% of those Americans were experiencing layoff anxiety.[24] With the possibility of job loss getting higher in this uncertain economic climate, any additional income source can help you deal with these uncertainties and give yourself the cushion you need.

Paying for college

Whether you're a parent trying to save up for your kid's college education or a young professional trying to pay off your student loan debt, having extra sources of income can definitely ease the burden and help you better manage these financial strains.

Live the lifestyle you want

Trying to live within your means, you may have sacrificed more by cutting your spending and limiting your options. If you don't want that anymore, your best bet is to create more sources of income and achieve your ideal lifestyle, which may not necessarily mean more luxury but at least more choice, comfort, and freedom.

Pay cash for purchases

You may have had to rely on credit whenever you had to repair or renovate something at home or make big purchases like buying a car. Having more income streams means more funds and savings, and that could help you ditch the loans and pay zero interest to keep more of your money!

Pay down debt

Paying a lot of interest from the multiple debts you have is getting in the way of your financial goals. Having more than one source of income can help you manage your debt by making extra payments every month. Feel free to review Chapter 5 if you are still in the process of paying off bad debt.

Diversify income sources

You may have heard this quote multiple times, "Don't put all your eggs in one basket". Diversifying your investments is always a great idea, but to do that, you need more money to build a diversified portfolio. If you start a hobby business and decide to use all the profits from it— no matter how little— for income diversification, that is an amazing step in the right direction!

Build a holiday fund

Some people with multiple income streams designate one source of income for leisure and holiday funds. This also helps you avoid using your credit card to pay for vacations and have the luxury of choice in terms of where and when you want to travel.

Take control of income

If you're solely relying on employment with no other income source, you'd have to actually wait for a pay raise before you could increase your income. That doesn't have to be the case. There are a lot of ways to take control of your income and give yourself the pay raise that you want, need, and most likely deserve!

Let's face it. Having more money can definitely solve a lot of your problems. To achieve financial security and design the life that you want, commit yourself *today* to start creating multiple streams of income.

COMMON MISTAKES WHEN CREATING MULTIPLE STREAMS

When committed to this, you can't just jump in without a plan or strategy. To ensure that your time and efforts will pay off, avoid the common mistakes people make and find an approach that will work best for you.

Watch out for these common pitfalls among those who try but fail (it is really awesome to learn from other peoples' mistakes!):

MISTAKE #1: Lack of Focus

When it comes to income sources, the more the better. However, when you're starting out, there's no harm or shame in doing it one step at a time. Instead of being random and aimless, be focused and strategic. Develop a plan that's more sustainable to avoid wasting time, money, and energy. Remember that more income streams can also mean more responsibilities. Focus and be intentional to avoid overwhelming yourself and wasting your efforts. It's better to do one thing at a time and generate results than to do everything all at once and fail to see real progress. Start by committing 3 hours a week to researching your next income stream.

MISTAKE #2: Not being intentional

As mentioned, there are multiple options and multiple industries you can position yourself in. The problem is not the lack of options and opportunities. The challenge lies in choosing the exact pursuit that belongs to you. While money is a great motivation, what if there comes a time when it no longer motivates you as much? While you're still starting out, it's best to give more thought to choosing your journey. It's best to choose a path that matches your skills, passions, and capabilities. Be intentional about this right from the start to ensure a more sustainable and enjoyable process.

MISTAKE #3: Working hard, not smart

I get it. Your results are proportional to your efforts, and if you don't have a lot of money to invest, you would need to work harder to earn more. While hard work is gold, you also need to work smart and take the time to think about the most efficient way to achieve your goals. A lot of people fail to work smart because they fail to think harder. The easy way is to 'do' and act right away, but high-quality action only comes from 'high-quality thinking'. Make sure to work smarter by strategizing your journey and following a course and a pace that works best for you.

MISTAKE #4: Not trusting and relying on other people

According to Roger James Hamilton, founder of the Entrepreneurs Institute, "Success comes from growing teams, not streams: multiple teams of income." If you intend to make it big, you can't go it alone. If you do everything by yourself, you'll only spread yourself too thin and burn out. One way to work smarter is by delegating some of the tasks to other people through outsourcing and building your dream team.

MISTAKE #5: Failing to save and invest

The point of multiplying your income stream is *not* to have more money to spend *but rather*, more money to save and invest! While we talked about improving your lifestyle as one of the reasons for increasing your income, you want to fuel the exponential growth of your finances by investing consistently. The more you save and invest every month, the faster you can achieve big and meaningful goals like paying cash for that fancy car, or early retirement.

MISTAKE #6: Comparing your results to others

Remember: Don't compare your Chapter 1 to someone else's Chapter 10. You are still starting out in your journey to financial freedom, and those self-made millionaires who are already raking in huge successes have also started from the bottom. *Respect the journey by trusting the process.* Your efforts are just as important as your results. It takes time to build the ideal outcomes, but the good news is you have already started!

CONCLUSION

Having multiple income streams brings both financial freedom, security, and peace of mind. Good thing we now live in a world with boundless opportunities and possibilities. It's now easier than ever to grab opportunities and get your side hustles spun up while you're still young.

THE REAL WORLD . . . Listen to the story of young Logan Allec. When he was 21 years old, he had $35,000 debt, zero bank account balance, and no car. He felt like he was in a rather hopeless situation. He sat in his cubicle one morning, realizing how his future will always remain dim and chaotic if he doesn't take deliberate action. Then and there, he decided that the only way to start improving his situation is by boosting his income and lowering his expenses. He worked as much overtime as possible and took on side hustles. He lowered his expenses by sharing a room with three other guys, saving him $275 per month. He stopped eating out so much and went for generic items at the supermarket instead of the brand name ones. Fast forward 18 months and he had $10,000 in savings and added $2000 to his bank account every month. He continues to expand his side hustles so as to cut back on the overtime.[38] With this new financial mindset, he is unstoppable!

6 PITFALLS TO AVOID

- Lack of focus
- Not being intentional
- Working to hard, and not smart enough
- Not trusting and relying on other people
- Failing to save and invest
- Comparing your results to others

KEY TAKEAWAYS

1. According to the IRS, the average millionaire has at least 7 streams of income. There are a lot of ways to earn more, but it's best to work smart and focus on building passive income sources.

2. With the rising healthcare costs, layoff possibilities, costs of education, excessive debt, and other economic uncertainties, having multiple sources of income can be the cushion you need to sleep better at night.

3. When it comes to building multiple income streams, you don't have to rush. You just have to start and be consistent in your journey to financial freedom.

EXERCISE

As the Buddha says 'A jug fills drop by drop'. While you can't have all 7 income streams millionaires have right away, you can work towards them one step at a time. In this exercise, choose any one of the following, and take that first step! Remember to commit 3 hours (or more) per week to this endeavor.

- Switch to a better-paying job or ask for a raise.
- Offer your services as a freelancer on Fiverr or Upwork.
- Invest $200 every month in dividend-paying stocks.
- Save up for a down payment on a house or your first rental property.
- Start and finish the book, app, game, or whatever creation you have long wanted to work on.
- Start a side business, be it a product-based, service-based, franchise, or an online business.

The greatest journeys all start with a single step. Take that step today and never look back. You've got this!

Chapter 7

PAYING TAXES

---

*T*axes have been a default governmental component for over 5,000 years and serve as the backbone to mobilize governments and their initiatives.[26] Taxes can definitely eat up a huge portion of your salary, but running a country is also not cheap, and governments have to rely on income tax and other forms of taxation to perform various civil operations.

THE IMPORTANCE OF TAXES

Simply put, without taxes, a nation will fall into social collapse. From funding public services to maintaining law and order, taxes are the foundation of our modern society. Let's emphasize the role of taxes in the following key aspects:

Governance
A government cannot function without taxes. Public goods and services require funding. Historically, the two most fundamental responsibilities of government is to secure the borders and provide for the defense of the citizenry. From general law and order to judicial systems and administrative services, taxation plays a vital role in funding governance.

Education

Tax revenue funds state schools, colleges, and educational institutions. It supports educational resources, research initiatives, infrastructure development, and public school teachers' salaries as well. America is all about democracy, fairness, and equal opportunity, and public education helps preserve such ideals.

On a macro-level, the government's educational spending also has other ripple effects besides trying to uphold good quality education. It also stimulates the local economy by creating more jobs and giving opportunities to building contractors, office suppliers, food vendors, and other school service providers.

Health

Tax revenue is used for building public hospitals and clinics, conducting medical research, sourcing medical equipment, and employing public healthcare professionals. The government also initiates disease prevention campaigns, vaccination programs, and health education initiatives to boost general public health.

REASONS WHY EVERYONE SHOULD PAY TAXES

Paying taxes is our civic duty and is a requirement of the law. Since we belong to a civilized society, not following the law could mean penalties, fines, or even jail time. Although we do want to pay less taxes and the government obviously isn't perfect, our tax dollars go to many places. The following are the main reasons we should pay taxes:

Funding the government

Without taxes, it's impossible for a government to run a country. Income tax is one of the biggest income sources of any government. Some people think of it as a burden, but it is actually crucial to secure a country's stability. The best scenario is when the populous are vigilant observers of governance to ensure efficiency and proper scope, i.e the philosophy of "subsidiarity" is essential here. Subsidiarity simply means that what can be handled at the local level, should be handed at the local level, and *not* be kicked up to, or subsumed into the larger, less local governing body.

Contribute to national programs

The US has many programs that contribute to the flourishing of the nation. These include:

- National Defense
- Agriculture and natural resources
- National Parks
- Law enforcement
- Science and medical research
- International affairs
- Energy and utility subsidies
- Education and childcare assistance
- Training services
- Community development
- Social security programs
- Education services

The list goes on. You are playing a role in making these programs possible. Although it's not always easy to see the big picture, there is a big picture. That is why taxes are regarded as the 'necessary evil'.

The big question is, are the tax dollars we're paying successfully supporting that big picture? Unfortunately, that is debatable in the United States and in many developed countries.

Oftentimes, the government is so huge it makes decision-making and coordination for many activities extra challenging. There are overlaps and duplications that need to be addressed. With the sheer size of the federal government, it's also difficult for private watchdogs, federal auditors, and oversight committees to monitor and regulate all the government spending. Our federal government funds over 2,200 benefit programs and subsidies, and these are all susceptible to fraud, waste, and abuse.

According to Open the Books, in 2022, the federal government wasted an average of $683 million per day.[34] The following are the government departments that are deemed most wasteful:

- Department of Health and Human Services
- Small Business Administration's Paycheck Protection Program
- Treasury Department
- Department of Defense
- Internal Revenue Service
- Transportation Security Administration
- Environmental Protection Agency

The government's wasteful spending is all due to inefficient management, excessive spending, and the system's inherent vulnerability to fraud and abuse. For example, between 2003 and 2001, the Washington Metropolitan Area Transit Authority wasted $416,789 just to maintain a self-cleaning toilet. In 2008, California taxpayers spent $9 billion on a high-speed rail project connecting Los Angeles and San Francisco that actually cost $33 billion to be operational in 2020. Due primarily to mismanagement, the project is delayed 15 years and the new estimated cost is $105 billion. The first phase of the rail project won't even be ready until 2029.[35] There are many examples of wasteful spending across many government departments and programs.

The only real solution is to downsize this massive government. The funds and decision-making should be decentralized out of Washington. Responsibilities and duties should be handed to state governments, and relevant federal activities should be privatized for further efficiency. Again, subsidiarity comes into play. Centralization only benefits politicians, and over the years of inefficient governance, the US taxpayers have become more alienated from the federal government, sickened by its corruption and dysfunction.

WHAT YOUNG ADULT NEEDS TO KNOW ABOUT TAXES

Filing your taxes is a big milestone as you step into adulthood. Tax is everywhere, and it's important that you understand taxes to manage your personal finances well and avoid penalties and legal issues.

Filing tax returns

Filing taxes might seem complicated and taxing, but it's a part of your financial responsibility and a mark of independent living. Before filing your tax returns, gather all required documents.

You may not need every single one of these the first time you file taxes, but it's better to secure everything you might need.

Documents to Secure:

- **Social security number**
- **Bank account number:** In case there's a tax refund and you need to provide the bank account you'd like it to go
- **W-2 form:** If you're an employee, you can get this form from your employer.
- **1099 form:** This is for Independent contractors, subcontractors, and sole proprietors. They may also have to present their income statement, which may include 1099-K and 1099-Misc.
- **Income from investments:** If you have investments, cryptocurrency, or virtual transactions, secure the necessary records and documents. These may include 1099-B, 1099-INT, and 1099-DIV.
- **Receipts:** If you made donations, secure the receipts. If you're an independent contractor, make sure to keep all business-related receipts as well, including receipts for business expenses.
- **1099-G form:** If you've received unemployment payments during the year, you'll have to secure a 1099-G form.

- **1098-E form:** This document shows the amount of interest paid on your student debts during the year.
- **1098 mortgage interest form:** For homeowners, they would have to submit this form to show how much interest they've paid on their home loan during the year.
- **Property tax records (including your car)**
- **Healthcare coverage tax form:** If you or your household members signed up for healthcare coverage via the Affordable Care Act marketplace, you'll be required to submit a health care tax form like a 1095-A, -B or -C.

Options for Filing Tax Returns

There are many ways to file tax returns. These are the following:

- Directly using IRS tax forms
- Via tax filing software
- With the help of an accountant

If you choose to file your tax return yourself, it can get a bit overwhelming if it's your first time. It's usually easier to use tax filing software or hire an accountant.

If you want to use tax software, the following are great options:

- TurboTax
- H&R Block
- TaxAct
- TaxSlayer

They're relatively easy to use, and the software will walk you through every step. The IRS also has a program called FreeFile which around 70% of taxpayers are eligible to use for free.[27] Other free basic tax preparation services from the IRS include Tax Counseling for the Elderly and Volunteer Income Tax Assistance. This is where tax experts gather and volunteer to help the elderly and low-income families file their tax returns.

When Are Taxes Due?

Tax Day for Americans is the 15th of April. However, if the 15th falls on a public holiday or a weekend, it is moved to the following Monday. The taxes due on Tax Day are those from the previous calendar year ending on December 31.

Your W-2 and other essential tax documents usually start arriving by mail or become accessible online every January. If you're expecting a refund, file your tax return as soon as possible to get the money back earlier as well. If you owe more money, you have until Tax Day to pay the deficit.

Tax refund

You don't usually know in advance if you have a refund or if you owe more. Tax laws also tend to change, so if you got a refund the previous year, there's no guarantee that you'll also get another refund this year. If there's indeed a refund, you also don't know if the amount is going to be similar to the year prior. You can receive less refund or even owe more. Thus, it's best to:

- Secure a cushion of funds to afford paying your taxes in case you owe more
- Don't assume that you'll get a refund
- Never spend a refund before you even get the money

Other Things to Keep in Mind

Here are other things to keep in mind to ensure that filing your tax returns goes as smoothly as possible:

Check if your parents are still claiming you as a dependent

Your parents could still be claiming you as a dependent especially if you're still in college, still living with them, or still receiving their financial support. Your parents will gain tax benefits if they include you as a dependent.

Before you file your tax return, ask your parents if they've indeed claimed you as a dependent and indicate that information as you file your tax return.

You may need to file a state tax return
If you're living in a state with state taxes, you would need to file a state tax return on top of the federal tax return. Some states impose a flat income tax rate for the entire state while some use graduated rates. Some states may also require state tax filing if your income goes above a certain threshold.

Every state has their own rules in terms of filing tax returns, so make sure you review the rules in the state where you live or work. If you're employed, you may also ask the HR department of your company to get access to updated information. You may also check your state's tax website and the IRS website to review the updated tax guide.

Know the tax distinction between Employee vs. Independent Contractor
Employees get the W-2 tax form and self-employed taxpayers get the 1099. If you are an employee with side gigs, you get both. Filing tax returns can be more complicated as an independent contractor. There are additional forms to submit and you need to file estimated taxes on a regular basis as well. The big chunk independent contractors pay on or before Tax Day is the self-employment taxes. These are equivalent to Medicare and Social Security taxes employees pay. However, employees have employers that cover half of this cost. As a self-employed professional, you'll pay 100% of the total amount.

Know the corresponding benefits of direct employment vs independent contracting
Employees can be eligible for certain benefits like tax-favored retirement plans, health plans, and other employee benefits. Independent contractors may also qualify for certain benefit programs. They can also deduct business-related expenses to reduce their taxable income.

If they operate in a home office, there's also a home office deduction that can cover a portion of their home expenses like rent/mortgage, maintenance, and utilities. We'll explore more of these tax deductions in the next few pages.

Consider hiring a tax professional
Filing your own tax return is definitely doable, but it can get time-consuming. If you don't have much free time and you can afford to hire a tax professional, this can also be a good decision as a young adult. Not only are you making things easy, but you're also investing in knowledge by making the most of your accountant's expertise. This way, you can ask questions from an expert and understand what's going on. You can hire a certified public account or an enrolled agent. Ask for family and friends for recommendations as they may be able to offer a discount if you're vetted by a friend or family member.

MISTAKES TO AVOID

When filing tax returns, you need to be careful and thorough. If not, it can cost you money or make you miss out on a bigger refund. Here are some mistakes to avoid when preparing taxes:

1. **Not starting early and missing the deadline.** Don't wait for deadlines to come around. Start sorting things out as early as January or well before Tax Day. That way, you have enough time to secure all the forms and know all the numbers. If you start late and end up missing the deadline, you may have to incur penalties.

2. **Presenting incorrect or incomplete information.** This is actually one of the common mistakes of taxpayers, and this is also a result of not preparing early thus leaving little to no time to review the forms and ensure correct and complete data. Math errors are

very common, especially if done manually. That's why it's also easier to use software to minimize such errors.

3. **Deliberately not declaring your full income.** Some people make the mistake of not declaring all income earned. You are legally required to report all of your income, and not doing so may run the risk of being audited. If inaccuracies or inconsistencies are detected, that could lead to fines and/or penalties. Report all sources of income including those from side hustles, investments, and part-time jobs.

4. **Not keeping records diligently.** It's a good and helpful habit to keep all the records that could support the items you wish to claim on your tax return. Keep those receipts and organize your documents well to avoid chaos and ease into the tax season seamlessly.

5. **Not using refund money well.** Tax refunds usually call for a celebration, and some people even call it 'free money'. When in fact, it also just means you've made a mistake filling out your W-4 form and you happened to withhold more money than necessary. You might consider updating your W-4 form as withholding too much is equivalent to loaning the IRS money at 0% interest!

   One simple tool is to decide before you start preparing your taxes how you will allocate your refund, should you get one. Go ahead and take 30% for fun money and divy up the rest between investment and debt payment. This is a simple and smart strategy which gives you freedom to enjoy the refund as well as building wealth!

6. **Not paying the money you owe.** Perhaps the money withheld was not enough. In that case, you owe the IRS on Tax Day, and you have to pay for the remaining taxes you owe.

What to do if you can't pay your taxes

If you owe the IRS taxes but cannot afford to pay them, you still have to file your tax return before Tax Day and just pay as much as you can afford. If you don't file the tax return, you'll just owe more money by incurring a late filing penalty.

You can actually resort to an installment payment plan by attaching Form 9465 to the front part of your tax return and see if you can qualify. You would most likely be able to qualify if you owe less than $25,000 and can pay the amount in less than 5 years. On the 9465 form, state your proposed monthly payment as well as the dates you wish to make your monthly payments.

If an installment payment plan is still not a viable option, you can submit Form 433A and Form 656 to apply for "offer in compromise." If you qualify, you can settle the tax debt for less than the total amount owed. The IRS will investigate and check your financial situation and future income potential to gauge your eligibility.

Just remember that all of us have the obligation to pay taxes. To avoid unwanted trouble, it's best to prepare ahead of time, plan for how you want to file your tax return, gather the necessary documentation diligently, and consider asking for help from family and friends or from a tax professional. Just do what you ought to do and learn the ropes slowly but surely.

TAX DEDUCTIONS AND CREDITS FOR YOUNG ADULTS

There are ways you can reduce your taxable income or tax bill through tax deductions or tax credits. Let's explore all the tax deductions and credits you can maximize.

Tax deductions for young adults

Like any other generation of taxpayers, young adults are also able to de-duct various expenses on their taxes. This depends on the nature of the expenses and the taxpayer's overall eligibility. The following are some of the common tax deductions you can make the most of:

- **Student loan interest**
  Those who are funding their education or their child's education via student loans can be eligible for student loan interest tax benefit. They can deduct up to $2,500 worth of interest they paid for the year.

- **Mortgage interest for homeowners**
  Mortgage interest can also be deductible. Make sure you're keeping good records of your mortgage payments to further reduce your tax bill. You can deduct mortgage interest on the first $750,000 of mortgage debt you paid during the tax year. If you're married, the amount is halved at $375,000 for married couples filing separately.

- **Real estate tax**
  Your foreign, local, or state taxes are also deductible from your federal income taxes as long as they're levied for the general public welfare. Taxes charged for home renovation or home maintenance services like trash collection are not included.

- **Tax on vehicles, motorcycles, and boats**
  You can also deduct the sales tax on your vehicle purchases like motorcycles, cars, boats, motor homes, and even airplanes. However, this is only for the state and local tax, and there's a limit of $10,000.[29]

- **State and local income taxes (or sales taxes, at the taxpayer's option)**
  You can deduct either your income tax or sales tax but not both. The maximum deduction is $10,000. Many people choose to deduct their income tax because that usually exceeds their sales tax.

- **Charitable contributions**
  The standard deduction for a single person has been raised to $12,000. Standard deduction refers to the amount a taxpayer is allowed to subtract from the adjusted gross income. Your charitable contributions should be higher than $12,000 to claim the deductions. If this is too steep for you, one strategy you can follow is called "bunching". For example, instead of donating $6000 per year, you can double donate at little over $12000 every other year, ideally on a December to cover the current year and the following year.

Other Deductions

Cell phone deductions
Whether you're employed or self-employed, you may be using your personal cell phone a lot for business-related activities. For direct employment, though, cell phone expenses are only deductible if it's more than 2% of your adjusted gross income.

Continuing education or professional expenses
If you're spending money to advance your education and skills, that could also be tax deductible. It can be tax deductible as long as:

- It enables you to maintain or enhance your job skills
- It's required by law to keep your status like a real estate agent required to complete a certain number of hours of continuing education to renew their license.
- It's relevant to your current business. If it's an education expense for establishing a 'new' business, that is not eligible.

Education expenses may include school tuition, course fees, books, educational supplies, transportation, license renewal fees, industry podcast subscriptions, industry magazine subscriptions, etc.

Side-job expenses

More and more young adults engage in side gigs to earn extra income. While that means increasing your tax bill, your expenses for carrying out your side jobs can also be deductible. Just make sure to keep the records of those expenses to support your case: office equipment, computer, camera, tools, etc

Paying medical expenses for an aging parent

If you can claim your aging parent as your dependent, the medical expenses can be deducted against your taxable income. For your parent to qualify as a dependent, your parent must not have earned more than the gross income test limit for that year. The amount varies from year to year. In 2022, the gross income limit is $4,400. Social security income generally doesn't count.

Clothing deductions

Work clothes can be deductible if it's more than 2% of your adjusted gross income. Just include it under the "miscellaneous itemized deductions" on your tax return's Schedule A attachment.

Deductions for the Self-Employed

We mentioned in the previous pages how self-employed individuals have certain tax benefits. The following are the main ones:

Startup costs

Your capital expenses can be tax deductible– up to $5000 deduction. These expenses include market research, business travel, equipment, marketing, attorney fees, accountant fees, and so on. If you're setting up an LLC or a corporation, the maximum deduction could be up to twice higher.[30]

Part of self-employment tax

As mentioned in the previous pages, self-employed people pay the full Social Security and Medicare taxes since they don't have an employer to share the burden with. The good thing is 50% of that self-employment tax is deductible against their self-employment income. This only makes sense, because you are the employer! For example, a $1000 self-employment tax can reduce your taxable income by $500.

Self-employed retirement plan contributions

For self-employed taxpayers, your contributions to the following account options can be tax deductible although there can be certain annual limits:

- Simplified Employee Pensions (SEP)
- Savings Incentive Match Plan for Employees (SIMPLE)
- Solo 401(k)

Home office deduction

Whether you own or rent the place where you exclusively or regularly work, it can be categorized as a home office expense that is deductible against your taxable income. Home office expenses include your rent/mortgage interest, utilities, homeowners insurance, repairs, etc. If your home office covers 20% of your residential space, 20% of your yearly residential expenses can also be tax deductible.

Tax Credits for Young Adults

Tax credit refers to the amount you can directly subtract from the taxes you owe. The following are some of the tax credits you can qualify for:

The child tax credit

If you have children 17 years old or below as of the end of the year, there's a $2000 tax credit per qualifying child. The parent should meet the minimum earned income of $2500.

The American Opportunity and Lifetime Learning Credits

This tax credit applies to the first four years of postsecondary education. The maximum annual tax credit for AOTC is $2500. If the student is a dependent, their parents can claim the credit.

Child and Dependent Care Credit

CDCC is the tax credit parents or caregivers can claim. This is to help cover the costs of daycare or elderly care. The Child and Dependent Care credit can be up to $2000 per qualifying dependent.

The Earned Income Credit

This tax credit is for those with low earnings. This also helps offset the burden of Social Security taxes. This is a refundable credit which means that if the total credit is bigger than the tax you owe, the excess amount can be refunded. The exact credit amount depends on your income, filing status, and number of qualifying children.

Tax credits and deductions are crucial components of the overall tax system. Make sure that you're making the most of the available opportunities for reducing tax liability. Any amount you get to save from these credits or deductions could mean financial relief or could be used for achieving your financial goals.

CONCLUSION

Taxation is really not just a matter of financial responsibility, but it's a core pillar of our modern society. Paying taxes fuels our governments and upholds public welfare. We're all contributing to building a functioning system built for the common good. We've done our part, and we can only hope that the government will properly do theirs. Don't forget the lessons from the previous chapter, building multiple income streams. As these streams grow, you may need to register one or more business entities, at that point you would do well to consult a tax expert as your situation will be more complex.

THE REAL WORLD . . . And the next time you get a tax refund, think about ways to grow that money. Be inspired by the story of Diana Young. She immigrated to the US in 1989 and found work in the cleaning industry. In 2014, she received a $2,200 tax refund. She took a leap of faith and invested the money in building her own company, Transcend Maintenance Services, Inc. Her company is now an SBA-certified janitorial service provider serving clients across the state![39] What an inspiration!

6 TAX MISTAKES TO AVOID

- Missing the tax deadline
- Presenting incomplete or incorrect information
- Not declaring the full income
- Not using refund money well
- Failing to keep records diligently
- Not paying the money you owe

KEY TAKEAWAYS

1. Without taxes, a nation will fall into social collapse.

2. Since we belong to a civilized society, not following the law could mean penalties, fines, or even jail time.

3. As a taxpayer, you're playing a role in making the government's programs possible and successful. Although it's not always easy to see the big picture, there is a big picture.

EXERCISE

1. Review the tax deductions and tax credits listed below.

2. List all the deductions and credits that you think you qualify for.

3. Secure the necessary requirements, documents, or supporting evidence to be eligible for such credits and deductions.

4. Put a checkmark next to the item whose requirements you have taken care of.

TAX DEDUCTIONS

- Student loan interest
- Mortgage interest for homeowners
- Real estate tax
- Tax on vehicles, motorcycles, and boats
- State and local income/sales taxes
- Charitable contributions
- Cell phone deductions
- Continuing education or professional expenses:
- Side-job expenses
- Paying medical expenses for an aging parent
- Clothing deductions

For self-employed

- Startup costs
- Self-employed retirement plan contributions
- Home Office Deduction

TAX CREDITS

- Child tax credit
- American Opportunity and Lifetime Learning Credits
- Child and Dependent Care Credit
- Earned Income Credit

Stay diligent about keeping good records until the next Tax Day comes. You've got this!

Chapter 8

RETIREMENT PLANNING STRATEGIES

Retirement might seem like a distant thing you shouldn't worry about. Young generations' battle cry these days are 'YOLO' or 'You Only Live Once' and 'Invest in experiences'. While these can all be valid, and it is important to enjoy and capture the experience of the present, it doesn't have to get in the way of securing a comfortable life in the future. Every dollar you haphazardly spend on a fabulous dining experience or a luxurious holiday is a dollar taken away from your retirement account.

In this chapter, let's delve into the importance of retirement planning and the strategies you can follow to make the process manageable for you as a young adult trying to navigate the subtle intricacies of life.

WHY SAVE FOR RETIREMENT IN YOUR 20'S?

If regular retirement may seem too distant for you, perhaps what can motivate you as a young adult is the prospect of 'early retirement'. Perhaps you are working on a job you quite don't love, and there are other passions and pursuits you want to engage in, but the necessity of survival is holding you back.

Early retirement is probably one of the most worthwhile goals you can set and work towards achieving. Being 'work-optional' is a powerful thing. It means freedom to do what you want without having to worry about how you'd get by. Achieving early retirement means achieving financial freedom. Financial freedom is time freedom, and among all kinds of goals one can set in this world, I 100% believe that pursuing financial freedom is one of the best decisions you can make. You're earning your right to 'thrive' instead of just 'survive'. Financial freedom or early retirement, in the simplest terms, is when your passive income can cover your basic expenses, and to achieve that, you need some solid planning as early as today.

KNOW YOUR GOALS

Solid goal-setting requires being very specific about what you want to achieve. You can't just say 'I want to retire' or 'I want more money' Truly intentional goals follow the SMART formula:

- Specific
- Measurable
- Attainable
- Relevant
- Time-bound

Retirement is a long-term goal, and to make it more achievable and manageable, you can break it down to short-term goals. For example:

Long-term goal: Retire when I'm 45 years old

Short-term goals to achieve the long-term goal:
If you are 25 years old and you still have 20 years before the target retirement age, your short-term goals may look like this:

Short-term Goal #1:
For 2 hours a week, plan how to increase my income and reduce my expenses in such a way that I can save at least $1,500 per month (most probably will be a combination of reducing expenses and increasing

income). Recall the two eighteen year olds who saved up for 6 months to buy their first rental property. If they can do it, so can you!

Once you successfully save your target amount consistently and accumulate more money, you may decide to secure a rental property to help you expedite your early retirement goal. The next short-term goal could be:

Short-term Goal #2:
Find a property in a good location and as soon as you can secure the down payment, buy it and make it your first rental property (make sure that you eliminate consumer debt and secure your emergency fund before you secure the down payment).

Along the journey towards achieving a long-term goal, you can set multiple short-term goals according to how life transpires. You can change your approach as life unfolds (marriage, kids, etc), but keep the big goal static and keep your eye on the prize.

You need to know where you are, where you want to be, and how much you need to save up and invest to achieve your target retirement age and lifestyle.

COMPOUND INTEREST IS YOUR FRIEND

There are many ways to achieve early retirement or enjoy your ideal retirement lifestyle down the road. Review Chapter 6 about creating multiple streams of income. Managing to earn more today allows you to save and invest more. With compound interest, your money creates more money, and it's an exponential growth that can help you achieve your retirement goals in due time.

Here's an example of compound interest at work:

Let's say you invest $5000 in a safe long-term bond earning 3% interest per year. In the first year, your investment grows by 3%, which is $150. Your total investment is now $5,150. The following year, you earn another 3% interest. This time, you're getting 3% of $5,150. Your interest has grown by $154.5. Fast forward 25 years later and your total money will have more than doubled to $10,468.89.

You can expect more compound earnings if you invest in stock market, mutual funds, or other more growth-oriented investments as their year over year average growth is higher than 3%.

SAVING A LITTLE EARLY VS. SAVING A LOT LATER

If you're employed, make the most of your employer-based retirement plan. It's a tax-deferred investment, so all the more reason to put some money away to minimize taxes and give your money more time to grow. The employer match is also *free money*, consider it a raise! If you are not taking advantage of the employer match you are leaving $$ on the table. But at this point, you are too smart for that!

Let's cite a concrete example of the difference between saving a little early and saving a lot later:

A. You start saving early for as little as $100 a month with a yearly positive return of 12%, compounded monthly over 40 years.

B. Your friend only started investing 30 years later but can afford to invest as much as $1000 a month for 10 years, yielding the same return of 12%, compounded monthly.

Who do you think saves up more money in the end?

Your friend rakes in $230,000 *while you get more than $1.17 million.* Your friend invested 10 times more but chose to start late. Do not underestimate the power of compound interest. Allow your portfolio to grow and generate more by starting as early as now.

WHAT TO CONSIDER WHEN INVESTING

Investing is not just about the ability to save up and delay gratification. To fully maximize your earned income and increase your chances of creating passive wealth, you need the right strategies and investment plan to give your money the best chance to grow.

Your strategy depends on your goals. If you have short-term goals, you may want to maintain a higher level of liquidity to preserve your principal, but if you have long-term goals such as retirement, you would want to invest in assets that offer the best opportunity for growth.

When getting started, keep in mind the following considerations:

Market risk
Usually, the higher the return, the higher the level of risk, and the lower the rate of return, the lower the market risk as well. High-risk investments are those more prone to fluctuations. Examples of high-risk investments include cryptocurrency, private or startup equity, individual stocks, options and derivatives, and high-yield bonds. The low-risk ones include savings accounts, government bonds, index funds, REITs, dividend stocks, and blue-chip stocks.

Risk tolerance
How you invest depends on your risk tolerance. But generally, your risk tolerance and your confidence in your investing skills will get better with time and experience. Study all investment options there are. If you're just starting out, you may invest the majority of your funds in low-risk investment options and follow 'value investing strategies' instead of going speculative and putting all your resources in deals that are too good to be true. Once your portfolio grows, you can allocate a small percentage for more aggressive and high-yield opportunities.

Retirement horizon

This is central to developing your retirement and investing plan. You need to know your target retirement age and identify your specific long-term goal to know how much you need to invest every month and what risk tolerance you should be willing to adopt. You can also work with a financial advisor to establish a sound investment plan and retirement strategy suitable for your retirement goals, but be sure to ask about fee structure. You don;t want to get into the situation where your advisors fees are eating up all your gains!!

STRATEGIES FOR RETIREMENT

Most young adults want to focus on paying off their student loan debt first and feel like thinking about retirement is not yet relevant. However, you should keep in mind that it isn't just about securing a good retirement, strategizing and building long-term wealth is a way to make better financial decisions today and ensure that you're setting yourself up for success.

To make early retirement planning possible, these are the core strategies to follow.

Open a 401(k) account

401(k) is a straightforward payroll deduction, you won't even notice you're setting money aside for the future. Your 401(k) contributions get deducted from your salary before the federal government makes tax deductions. This type of tax-free savings is just something you shouldn't miss out on. You're minimizing losses and maximizing long-term gains. There are maximum limits to each 401(k) account, and if you can manage to max it out, you're setting out strong in your retirement planning journey. The IRS sets the maximum 410(k) contribution every year.

Many employers offer matching contributions. That means they would also contribute a percentage of your salary to your own 401(k) account. If your company has a 401(k) offering, all it takes to get started is some paperwork you need to fill out with the HR department. Once enrolled, you can choose a contribution amount and the investment funds you want your contributions to be allocated. You can also access and monitor your 401(k) contributions and progress online.

Maximize IRAs

While 401(k) is offered by employers, individuals can open their own IRAs via a bank or a broker. Like 401(k), IRAs including Roth IRAs are tax-free. IRAs have much lower yearly contribution limits, but you are free to have both 401(k) and IRA accounts, helping you further support your retirement goals.

Especially if your company doesn't offer a match, it's best to start with a Traditional IRA or Roth IRA and start 401(k) once you have already maxed out your IRA contributions. There's a much larger investment selection in IRA accounts and you can also avoid the administrative fees that some 401(k)s charge. If you're eligible, you can contribute to both Traditional IRA and Roth IRA, as long as you don't exceed the annual limits set by the IRS.

In the end, it's better to maximize as many retirement plans available to successfully drive your future financial success.

Buy life insurance

We just allocated an entire chapter of this book to highlight the importance of insurance, and it's always worth emphasizing. It's best to buy life insurance while you're still young while companies still see you as a healthy, low-risk customer. Because you are most likely in optimal health condition, you can receive cheaper monthly rates for your insurance plan. Not to mention the amount of time you're allowing your cash value to grow.

Open a health savings account (HSA)

HSA is another type of tax-advantaged account which enables you to put money aside for future medical expenses. Having an HSA account can also lower your monthly health insurance premiums. Unlike 401(k) wherein the withdrawals can be taxed, the gains and withdrawals of an HSA account remain tax-free. Like 401(k), the maximum annual contribution limits vary every year. If you can, stay away from a Flexible Spending Account (FSA) as any unspent money at the end of the year goes away and returns to your employer.

Invest in stocks/cryptocurrency

It's important to diversify your portfolio, and some of the good options include stocks and cryptocurrency. Crypto has been a debated topic in the financial world, but cryptocurrencies like Bitcoin and Dogecoin are already gaining mass adoption and mainstream credibility. While fiat or paper money loses value over time because of inflation, crypto is resistant to inflation because it's decentralized and is capped on supply. In terms of retirement and long-term goals, it can potentially yield lucrative returns.

You should also include investing in stocks, especially dividend investing, in your retirement strategy. We have talked about this in Chapter 6 when discussing multiple streams of income. Dividend investing is one of the main passive income streams of many millionaires, and it also doesn't require any large upfront cost. What matters is consistency and choosing the right companies with a proven track record and growth prospect.

TIPS FOR SAVING

Preparing and saving for retirement doesn't have to be intimidating if you apply the right tips and strategies. Let's discuss some of the things you can do to make saving for retirement more effective and manageable.

Save 10-15% a year

For young adults, experts advise saving 10-15% of your pre-tax income for retirement. The exact range depends on your preferred retirement lifestyle, your current income, and current expenses. If you want early retirement, you would have to find a way to increase that percentage to maybe 15-20%. For example, you may have heard of the FIRE or Financial Independence Retire Early movement. These devotees are saving up to 50% of their income to retire decades before the traditional retirement age. The FIRE movement is a program of aggressive savings and investment. There are two main steps to successfully pulling this off: (1) make a lot of money (2) save and invest a lot of money. FIRE devotees usually adopt minimalist living or embrace delayed gratification in order to aggressively pursue the lofty dream of early retirement. A large component of this approach is to have the social support of others committed to this cause. You may want to join a local FIRE group (in person or on-line) to see if this is for you.

Save for the bigger expenses

We talked a lot about saving, budgeting, and delayed gratification in the previous chapters, and I will have to highlight again the big role of savings in unlocking a secure and comfortable future. It may be hard to give up your daily coffee runs, but every little sacrifice will add up. Instead of draining your savings on random little purchases, be prepared to save up for the bigger ones including the following:

The 3 biggest spending categories in the typical American budget

- **Housing**
  Housing expenses usually eat up a third of the average budget. Another way to secure more savings is to avoid excessive housing costs and buy or rent only as much space as necessary. Choosing low-priced locations can also save you hundreds of dollars month after month.

- **Transportation**
  According to recent data from Kelley Blue Book, the average cost

of a new car in the US is $48,008.[31] To afford such a big purchase, consumers are taking out bigger loans to meet their transportation needs. When choosing a car, it's best to buy only what you need. Just opt for small or midsized vehicles that are more fuel-efficient and avoid upgrading your car every 2-3 years. Instead, keep it for the next 10-15 years and think about utility and practicality above all else. That is, if you are really serious about setting your finances up for success. Also consider living in a location that allows for easy use of public transportation.

- **Food**
  Americans waste about a third of the food they purchase.[32] The average mid-income household spends around 12% of their budget on food.[33] That means, around 4% of the average household budget goes to waste. When you save food, you're saving money as well. Make sure to buy only what you need, store food wisely, love your leftovers, and plan meals to reduce food waste at home.

Budget for a long retirement

For a comfortable and secure retirement, plan and prepare well. Ideally, leave the workforce or other income-generating activity only when you have enough resources to comfortably retire. *And have your passive income streams well established.*

In the corporate world, while it's okay to retire early, do remember that late retirement means more years of saving and it also means minimizing the chance of having to cut back on your lifestyle after retirement. If you don't want late retirement, focus on building passive sources of income like what we have discussed in Chapter 6. Build a diversified portfolio of dividend income, rental income, interest income, etc. Having as many backup assets as possible allows you to ensure that your retirement funds outlive you.

Get help from a retirement planning expert

Retirement planning has a lot of moving parts, and if you want an expert guide, you can choose to work with a financial planner who can help you come up with a thorough retirement analysis and strategy that works best for you. Financial planners have various fee structures, so be sure to understand that up front.

CONCLUSION

Some people consider retirement as a synonym of 'financial freedom'. *Essentially, retiring is just all about shifting your dependence from your paycheck to your portfolio.* Financial freedom is when your passive income exceeds your expenses, and you can achieve financial freedom decades before the usual retirement age as long as you focus on *building multiple passive income streams* and stay committed to *living strategically below your means*.

And remember: planning for retirement isn't just about securing money for the future but about living life on your own terms. It's about leading a full, meaningful life till your final years.

THE REAL WORLD . . . Let's look at the story of Jon Dulin. When he was in his 20's, he started reading books, blogs, and podcasts about personal finance. He realized all of them just say the exact same thing: *start saving and investing money.* So, he started. He squirreled money into his company's 401(k) plan and only saved $20 per paycheck. By the end of the year, he was surprised to see the tiny amounts he set aside already amounted to $1000 after dividends and growth.[38] This "experiment" propelled him into a totally new approach towards money, and the freedom that comes with saving, investing and growing your hard earned dollars!

5 RETIREMENT PLANNING MISTAKES TO AVOID

- Starting late in your retirement savings
- Not maximizing retirement plans
- Failing to secure life insurance
- Not diversifying your investment portfolio
- Not asking for expert advice when you need to

KEY TAKEAWAYS

1. Early retirement is probably one of the most worthwhile goals you can set or try to achieve. Being 'work-optional' is a powerful thing. It means freedom to do what you want without having to worry about how you'll get by.

2. With compound interest, your money creates more money, and it's an exponential growth system that can help you achieve your retirement goals in due time.

3. Maximize as many retirement plans available to successfully drive your future financial success.

EXERCISE

Follow the steps below to start mobilizing your retirement goals! Feel free to put a checkmark beside each item you have initiated or completed.

1. Ask your HR department if your company offers matching contributions to 401(k). If yes, open a 401(k) account as soon as possible. If not, open an IRA account and max it out before you open a 401(k) account.

2. Buy life insurance while the monthly premiums are still cheaper.

3. Open a Health Savings Account (HSA).

4. Invest in dividend stocks and set a realistic amount you can commit to invest every month.

5. Go back to Chapter 6 and work on multiplying your income streams to boost your saving and investing potential and to build assets that can nourish your retirement years.

CONCLUSION

_____

*Y*our 20's are mainly all about finding the right balance between building the right foundation as an adult and enjoying life. This phase is also filled with a lot of milestones like moving for work, getting married, buying a home, and having children. And while life shouldn't be taken too seriously, there's also zero drawback and every advantage in taking control of your finances as early as today.

In this book, we talked about a lot of things that sum up a financially healthy lifestyle. Let's try to review some of the biggest **takeaways**.

At the beginning of the book, we talked about the importance of knowing your **financial position**. You need to face your **financial situation head-on and be proactive about** eliminating your financial hurdles **one by** one. Every person has different **financial priorities, and I want to emphasize** this handy pyramid once more.

The base is the very foundation, which involves many concepts we have thoroughly discussed in this book. These include crucial

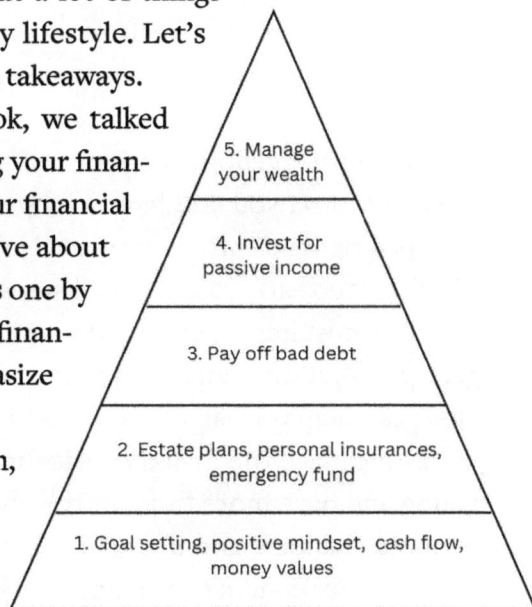

5. Manage your wealth

4. Invest for passive income

3. Pay off bad debt

2. Estate plans, personal insurances, emergency fund

1. Goal setting, positive mindset, cash flow, money values

fundamentals like guilt-free budgeting, self-discipline, and delayed gratification.

The second layer of the pyramid is all about *adding a layer of security* to your finances in the form of insurance and emergency funds.

The third step is paying off bad debt. We devoted an entire chapter to debt reduction and elimination, and we discussed different strategies for building credit, managing student loans, and avoiding the debt trap.

The fourth layer is passive income generation, which is what Chapter 6 is all about. We talked about the different ways to earn more income, especially passive income, such as stock dividends, real estate, royalties, business income, interest income, and capital gains. Successfully creating passive income and investing in retirement plans can help you fare well in the future. Building passive wealth also helps you retire early and allows for a 'work-optional' lifestyle. You will then have the freedom to pursue your truest passions and interests. We have only one life to live, and financial freedom can help you achieve what you are born to do.

The top of the pyramid is all about wealth management. The goal is to be wealthy and stay wealthy. As long as you sustain all your income streams and live below your means, your financial wealth will be unstoppable.

Financial freedom is a journey, and as a young adult committed to your future, you still have a long way to go. Even if you feel cash-strapped right now in an entry-level job and still trying to figure life out, it's never too early to take small steps towards financial security. Start with the most important foundations highlighted in this book like budgeting well, saving consistently, and avoiding debt. These simple things alone can help you carve your path toward success.

Don't make the mistake of feeling invincible because you're still young and have more time on your hands. Financial emergencies are bound to happen, and if you aren't ready, life won't care (remember the insurance commercial about "mayhem"?). Build an emergency fund, start thinking about retirement, and sort your finances out one aspect at a time. Commit to the process!

Money management is exciting! Directing your financial future is rewarding beyond belief. Financial freedom and the peace, comfort, and joy it brings into your life were almost unimaginable before picking up this book. Hopefully, at this point, you can see your freedom on the near horizon!

I hope that you have learned many new concepts, tools, and strategies about navigating life in your 20's. I truly wish you all the best on your journey. I know you're doing your very best, and I know you have what it takes to improve your finances and reach your biggest goals. Keep your eye on the prize, and never give up. You got this!

ENDNOTES

1   The State of Personal Finance Annual Report: Trends for 2023. *Ramsey Solutions*. https://www.ramseysolutions.com/budgeting/state-of-personal-finance

2   Jacobe, B. D. (2021, May 7). One in Three Americans Prepare a Detailed Household Budget. *Gallup.com*. https://news.gallup.com/poll/162872/one-three-americans-prepare-detailed-household-budget.aspx

3   Credit Card and Unsecured Personal Loan Balances Remain at or Near-Record Levels as Consumers Navigate Challenging Economic Climate. *Trans Union*. https://newsroom.transunion.com/q1-2023-ciir/

4   Ewald, François. 1991. *Insurance and risk*. In The Foucault Effect: Studies in Governmentality. *Chicago. University of Chicago Press,* ISBN: 978-0226080451.

5   National Safety Council Injury Facts (2021). Speeding. *National Safety Council*. https://injuryfacts.nsc.org/motor-vehicle/motor-vehicle-safety-issues/speeding/

6   Kaiser Family Foundation. (2022). Americans' Challenges with Health Care Costs. *Kaiser Family Foundation*. Retrieved from https://www.kff.org/health-costs/issue-brief/americans-challenges-with-health-care-costs/

7   National Association of Realtors (September 2021). The Impact of Student Loan Debt 2021. *National Association of Realtors*. https://cdn.nar.realtor/sites/default/files/documents/2021-the-impact-of-student-loan-debt-report-executive-summary-09-14-2021.pdf

8   Front Psychol 2020. Relationship Between Debt and Depression, Anxiety, Stress, or Suicide Ideation in Asia: A Systematic Review. *National Library of Medicine*. https://www.ncbi.nlm.nih.gov/pmc/articles/PMC7381269/

9 Alex Gailey (2023, May 8). More than half of Americans say money negatively impacts their mental health, up sharply from a year ago. *Bankrate*. https://www.bankrate.com/personal-finance/financial-wellness-survey/#inflation

10 AIMS Public Health. (2020). Problems paying medical bills and mental health symptoms post-Affordable Care Act. National Library of Medicine. https://www.ncbi.nlm.nih.gov/pmc/articles/PMC7327393/

11 Financial Security Program (2018, August 2). The Burden of Debt on Mental and Physical Health. *Aspen Institute*. https://www.aspeninstitute.org/blog-posts/hidden-costs-of-consumer-debt/

12 Risk and Protective Factors. *Centers for Disease Control and Prevention.* https://www.cdc.gov/suicide/factors/index.html

13 Press Release (2016). More than 1 in 4 Employers Do Not Conduct Background Checks of All New Employees. *Career Builder.* https://press.careerbuilder.com/2016-11-17-More-than-1-in-4-Employers-Do-Not-Conduct-Background-Checks-of-All-New-Employees-According-to-CareerBuilder-Survey

14 Richard Laycock (2023, May 8). Finder Consumer Confidence Index. *Finder*. https://www.finder.com/consumer-confidence-index

15 Tracy Kitten (2022, October 26). Child Identity Fraud: The Perils of Too Many Screens and Social Media. *Javelin*. https://javelinstrategy.com/whitepapers/child-identity-fraud-perils-too-many-screens-and-social-media

16 Erin El Issa (2021, June 14). 2021 Consumer Credit Card Report. *NerdWallet*. https://www.nerdwallet.com/article/credit-cards/2021-consumer-credit-card-report

17 Household Debt and Credit Report (Q1 2023). *Federal Reserve Bank of New York.* https://www.newyorkfed.org/microeconomics/hhdc

18 Nicole Dieker (2023, January 9). How credit inquiries affect your credit score. *Bankrate*. https://www.bankrate.com/personal-finance/credit/how-credit-inquiries-affect-credit-score/#multiple

19 Elizabeth Gravier (2022, August 26). Here's how the average student loan borrower can save literally thousands of dollars by refinancing. *CNBC*. https://www.cnbc.com/select/student-loan-refinancing-saves-money/

20 Bill Fay (2023, July 21).Demographics of Debt. *Debt*. https://www.debt.org/faqs/americans-in-debt/demographics/

21 Jenny Bourne and Lisa Rosenmerkel. Over the Top: How Tax Returns Show that the Very Rich Are Different from You and Me. *IRS*. https://www.irs.gov/pub/irs-soi/14rpoverthetopbournerosenmerkel.pdf

22 Katharina Buchholz, (2023, Feb 7). The U.S. Has the Most Expensive Healthcare in the World. *Statista*. https://www.statista.com/chart/8658/health-spending-per-capita/

23 Peter G. Peterson Foundation (2023, July 12). How Does the Us Healthcare System Compare to Other Countries.*PGPF*.https://www.pgpf.org/blog/2023/07/how-does-the-us-healthcare-system-compare-to-other-countries

24 Jack Flynn (2023, June 8). 20 Must-know Layoff Statistics [2023]: Who's Being Terminated From Their Jobs. *Zippia*. https://www.zippia.com/advice/layoff-statistics/

25 Courtney Gilbert and Steven Kirshblum (2020). Surfer's myelopathy: an atypical case presentation. *NCBI*. https://www.ncbi.nlm.nih.gov/pmc/articles/PMC7275076/#CR6

26 Tax Edu (2023). Tax Glossary. *Tax Foundation*. https://taxfoundation.org/taxedu/glossary/tax/

27 Carmen Reinicke (2022, February 8). Here's who can file taxes to the IRS for free this year. *CNBC*. https://www.cnbc.com/2022/02/08/heres-who-can-file-taxes-to-the-irs-for-free-this-year-.html

28 Tax information Center (2023). Is there a vehicle sales tax deduction? Can I deduct sales tax on a vehicle purchase. *H&R Block*. https://www.hrblock.com/tax-center/filing/adjustments-and-deductions/vehicle-sales-tax-deduction/

29 IRS (2023). About Publication 526, Charitable Contributions. *Internal Revenue Service*. https://www.irs.gov/forms-pubs/about-publication-526

30 IRS (2022). Publication 535, Business Expenses. *Internal Revenue Service.* https://www.irs.gov/publications/p535

31 Kelley Blue Book (2022, April 11). After Nearly Two Years, New-Vehicle Transaction Prices Fall Below Sticker Price in March 2023. *KBB.* https://b2b.kbb.com/news/view/new-vehicle-transaction-prices-march-2023/

32 John Wiley (2020, January 23). Estimating Food Waste as Household Production Inefficiency. *Wiley Online Library.* https://onlinelibrary.wiley.com/doi/10.1002/ajae.12036

33 USDA (2022, October 31). Food spending as a share of income declines as income rises. *United States Department of Agriculture.* https://www.ers.usda.gov/data-products/chart-gallery/gallery/chart-detail/?chartId=58372

34 Fox and Friends (2023, May 4). Government's most wasteful spending revealed as US nears debt limit. *Fox News.* https://www.foxnews.com/video/6326746590112

35 Ralph Vartabedian (2022, May 6). Governor, legislators won't budge in high-speed rail dispute. *Call Matters.* https://calmatters.org/politics/2022/05/california-high-speed-rail-standoff/

36 The Household Finances Deep Dive Edition (July 20213). New Reality Check: The Paycheck-to-paycheck Report. *Pymnts.* https://content.pymnts.com/wp-content/uploads/2023/07/PYMNTS-New-Reality-Check-July-2023.pdf

37 LearnVest (2015, July 3). 9 Inspiring Stories of Ultimate Financial Freedom. *Forbes.* https://www.forbes.com/sites/learnvest/2015/07/03/9-inspiring-stories-of-ultimate-financial-freedom/?sh=e4d2d9f1feac

38 Jackie Lam (2019, April 12). 4 Inspiring Stories to Motivate You to Become More Financially Literate. *Chime.* https://www.chime.com/blog/4-inspiring-stories-to-motivate-you-to-become-more-financially-literate/

39 Success Stories. Tax Refund Fueled Her American Dream. *U.S Small Business Administration.* https://www.sba.gov/success-story/tax-refund-fueled-her-american-dream

www.ingramcontent.com/pod-product-compliance
Lightning Source LLC
Chambersburg PA
CBHW030522210326
41597CB00013B/991

* 9 7 9 8 9 8 9 9 9 6 9 0 2 *